D0984046

The Community in
Rural America

This volume is one of a series of six studies to be published by Greenwood Press under the auspices of the Rural Sociological Society prepared to commemorate its fiftieth anniversary (1937–1987). Professor James J. Zuiches, of Washington State University, is the series editor. The topics covered by this series include community, natural resources, structure of agriculture, diffusion of innovations, population, and the history and social context of rural sociological research.

Published Titles

Rural Sociology and the Environment
Donald R. Field and William R. Burch, Jr.

Population and Community in Rural America
Lorraine Garkovich

The Sociology of Agriculture
Frederick H. Buttel, Olaf F. Larson, and Gilbert W. Gillespie, Jr.

THE COMMUNITY IN RURAL AMERICA

KENNETH P. WILKINSON

UNDER THE AUSPICES OF THE
RURAL SOCIOLOGICAL SOCIETY

Contributions in Sociology, Number 95

Greenwood Press
New York • Westport, Connecticut • London

Library of Congress Cataloging-in-Publication Data

Wilkinson, Kenneth P.
     The community in rural America / Kenneth P. Wilkinson ; under the
auspices of the Rural Sociological Society.
          p.   cm. — (Contributions in sociology, ISSN 0084-9278 ; no.
95)
     Includes bibliographical references and index.
     ISBN 0-313-26467-8 (alk. paper)
     1. United States—Rural conditions. 2. Rural development—United
States. 3. Sociology, Rural. 4. Community. I. Rural Sociological
Society. II. Title. III. Series.
HN59.2.W525   1991
307.72′0973—dc20   90-47534

British Library Cataloguing in Publication Data is available.

Library of Congress Catalog Card Number: 90-47534
ISBN: 0-313-26467-8   *ftw*
ISSN: 0084-9278
                             ADS 6001
First published in 1991

Greenwood Press, 88 Post Road West, Westport, CT   06881
An imprint of Greenwood Publishing Group, Inc.

Printed in the United States of America

∞

The paper used in this book complies with the
Permanent Paper Standard issued by the National
Information Standards Organization (Z39.48-1984).

10 9 8 7 6 5 4 3 2 1

This book is dedicated to
Harold Frederick Kaufman
(1911–1990)

Contents

Preface

The community is a venerable topic of research and teaching in rural sociology and a focus of continuing controversies in theory and policy. Sociologists have been debating the meaning and usefulness of such concepts as rural, community, and community development for many years. As happens from time to time, rural community development has recently surfaced as a keystone of proposals for a national rural development policy in the United States. As one might expect, however, trends in academic and policy debates are not always synchronous. Currently, sociologists are questioning the conventional concept of the community as a local society and asking whether rural community development is possible in an essentially urban world. Meanwhile, ignoring such questions, proponents of rural development at federal and state levels are arguing persuasively that community action and community leadership must be at the forefront of effective programs to address rural problems. The time is ripe for rural sociology, with its academic base in research and theory and its policy orientation, to come up with useful answers to some old questions. What is a community? How does community influence social well-being? How do communities develop? How do rural and urban characteristics of a population affect the prospects for community development and social well-being? What could be done to promote rural community development and rural well-being? The search for answers calls for a review of what is known and then for an agenda to guide future work.

As part of a series sponsored by the Rural Sociological Society, this review pulls together suggestions and findings from research on the community in rural America and outlines challenges for the future in rural sociology and rural policy. The idea that the community, whatever else it might be, is a process of local social interaction, provides the organizing theme for a critical analysis of theoretical, methodological, and policy issues. In building upon this theme, the book elaborates a theory of community interaction from concepts developed by Harold F. Kaufman, a community scholar and distinguished rural sociologist who also was a wonderful teacher. Detailed comments on earlier drafts of the manuscript by Willis J. Goudy, Edward W. Hassinger, Glenn D. Israel, and A. E. Luloff revealed numerous gaps and ambiguities and contributed greatly to clarification of the central argument. The patient and diligent encouragement of the series editor, James J. Zuiches, was of enormous value in nudging this project toward completion. Their efforts have aided my search for answers to key questions about the community in rural America.

The Community in
Rural America

Introduction: Studying the Community in Rural America

Community sociology has had its ups and downs over the past half century and so, it seems, has the community. Perhaps the sociology of the community has changed more in this century than have the fundamental qualities of the community itself, or at least that is a subject for debate and discussion. In any event, the sociology of community has changed. The tradition of community ethnographies of the first half of the twentieth century in Europe and the United States gave way in the 1960s to comparative statistical analyses of specific and limited aspects of community organization, and in the 1970s, to the study of phenomena in local societies that have little to do with community as such. In fact, by the end of the 1970s, some leading writers on social organization were ready to abandon the conventional concept of the community. Some sociologists would argue today that *community* is only a romantic term for a way of life long since passed in the progress of civilization. However, the scholarly literature is showing signs of a revival of interest in the community, especially in rural sociology, and community action has emerged again as an emphasis in rural policy. Whether this means the community itself is making a comeback remains to be seen.

Two of the major questions among those addressed in contemporary essays and research on this subject highlight the issues in the study of the community in rural areas. First, how is it possible for the community to persist in modern society? Second, how does ruralness affect this possibility? These questions relate to the essential elements of the concept of the community, and attempts to answer them can help to clarify those elements. A review of these questions provides an introduction to this study of the community in rural America.

Sociological approaches to these questions often emphasize some particular aspect of local social life more than other aspects. Ecological approaches emphasize adaptive mechanisms. Cultural studies concentrate on institutions and values. Organizational approaches examine structures and relationships that integrate a local society and relate it to the larger society. Social psychological studies measure community identification and satisfaction. In this study the emphasis is on social interaction, a pervasive feature of community life that underlies and gives substance to the ecological, cultural, organizational, and social psychological aspects. Interaction is thus a core property of the community, one without which community, as defined from virtually any sociological perspective, could not exist. Moreover, the interactional approach concentrates on an aspect of community that persists in modern society while other aspects appear to be losing their distinctiveness. For these reasons, an approach that emphasizes social interaction is most appropriate for understanding the influence of ruralness on community life in modern society.

Conventionally, there are three elements of the community, namely, a locality, a local society, and a process of locality-oriented collective actions. The third of these is the focus here and is termed "the community field" (Kaufman, 1959; Wilkinson, 1970b). A locality is a territory where people live and meet their daily needs together. A local society is a comprehensive network of associations for meeting common needs and expressing common interests. A community field is a process of interrelated actions through which residents express their common interest in the local society. While sociologically important units other than the community could embody one or two of these elements, the community, as used here, embodies all three elements.

This definition rules out a number of things we might call community in everyday language, or, for that matter, in sociology. A neighborhood, for example, is only part of a community, because a neighborhood by definition is not the whole of a local society. A gathering of like-minded scientists (or musicians or political activists or whatever) might be called a community, but it is not one by this definition. Similarly, people who think of themselves as a community do not necessarily constitute a community, unless they also live and act together in a local society. Moreover, the extent of community in a local society varies through time depending on the actions people take in response to local problems and opportunities. The combination with all three elements present delineates the community as a most distinctive sociological unit.

While this is a restrictive definition, it specifies a social entity that can play a vital role in human experience and well-being. Part of the importance of the community is its role as the setting and the mechanism of empirical contact between the individual and society. This is a crucial role because immediate social experience is necessary to social well-being. This is true because society is an abstraction one can experience only indirectly or symbolically. The empirical manifestation of society is interaction in localities. Contact with society occurs first in family and then, more comprehensively, in the community. The community also is important because of its role in meeting the needs of people, especially the needs for collective involvement and social definition of self. One meets these needs primarily through interactions and involvements in the local society. The quest for community, therefore, is a central theme in human history, past and present.

The view that the community is imperiled is an old, if not outmoded, one in sociology. Eighteenth- and nineteenth-century theories of societal transformation described the demise of the isolated close-knit community and its folk institutions in the face of the industrial revolution and the rise of capitalism. Emile

Durkheim, at the close of the nineteenth century, discussed the change from a pattern of communities integrated within themselves to a pattern of local integration into the larger society. Pitirim Sorokin, writing in the 1920s, established the transformation theory as a basic paradigm for rural sociology. Later, in the 1960s, Roland Warren popularized the view that a "great change" is altering the conventional bases of cohesion in local societies. In this latter paradigm, the community, as a complete and cohesive local society, is seen as a vestige of the old order.

In the third edition of *The Community in America*, for example, Warren (1978) observes that the community has become a turbulent arena of self-seeking actions and can no longer be understood as a concrete collectivity or system. Community interaction still occurs, he says, but the community as a systemic entity appears only sporadically and liaisons among major actors in the community arena tend to be short-lived.

Others, writing from a critical perspective, see capitalist development as the undoing of community, at least for the short run. The modern community, from this perspective, is organized and manipulated to facilitate the exploitation of labor and the accumulation of profits, although over the long run Marxian theory sees community as something to be achieved by society after the class dialectic comes to a head. Even without Marxian assumptions, many writers observe that capitalist development is divisive and that the community, as Harvey Molotch (1976) says, is a "growth machine" serving not the common good but the interests of those who manipulate that machine for profit.

Indeed, in a modern capitalist society one must be cautious about accepting apparent evidence of solidarity on face value. Such events as the erection of a community monument or the staging of an annual community celebration might be taken to indicate a strong bond of mutual identity and collective-mobilization potential in a local society, but closer examination sometimes reveals such events to be shams perpetrated by a self-interested elite for the purpose of masking class exploitation and domination.

Furthermore, as Barry Wellman argues in the introduction to his analysis of "The Community Question" (1979), the search for an all-embracing solidarity in a local society expresses a conservative value bias, or what he calls an obsession with order and control in American sociology. He argues that consensus among diverse segments of a complex local society can only be gained at the expense of freedom. Tolerance of diversity and open negotiation among conflicting interest groups would reduce the probability that community, as an area-wide phenomenon, could persist. Wellman thus poses his community question as an issue not in the overall network of social relationships in the locality but in intimate ties among people wherever these might occur in space.

From almost any perspective, one can find serious problems with each of the three elements of the conventional definition of the community. The *locality* today tends to have vaguely deline-ated boundaries and boundaries that overlap with those of other settlements. These boundaries, such as they are, also change rapidly as people move about over wide territories to meet their daily needs. The *local society* today is comprised in large part of units and branches of regional, national, and multinational orga-nizations. Firms, voluntary associations, and even individuals tend to be linked to social units outside the locality, and these extra-local connections can be stronger and more influential than the ties among groups and individuals within the local society. The field of *community action* perhaps is the most problematic of the three essential components of a community. As Charles Tilly (1973) says, "urbanization of the world" has sharply reduced the probability that communities will "act." By this he means the probability that collective behavior will express a widespread solidarity or identity of interest in the local society is reduced. Communities can still act, he says, but only under rare circumstances, such as when a community with a history of activeness experiences a pervasive threat to its dominance of the local territory.

If the boundaries are fuzzy, the local society is dominated by extra-local ties, and local action often expresses private rather than collective interests, why should we continue to search for the community? Why not focus our attention instead on those structures and involvements through which people now meet the needs they once met through community relationships?

The thesis of this study is that the community has not disappeared and has not ceased to be an important factor in individual and social well-being. People still live together in places, however fluid might be the boundaries of those places. They still encounter the larger society primarily through interactions in the local society. And, at crucial moments, they still can act together to express common interests in the place of residence. Local social life has become very complex in the typical case, but complexity and the turbulence associated with it do not in and of themselves rule out community.

There is considerable room for doubt that a major change has in fact occurred over the past century or so in the fundamental role of the community in American social life, notwithstanding dramatic changes in technology and culture and in many other aspects of social organization. As shown in historical analyses by Thomas Bender (1978) and Robert Richards (1978), the notion of a recent change from more to less local autonomy does not fit well with the facts of American history, although such a transition surely occurred earlier in Europe. Local communities have been tightly linked to large centers virtually from the beginning of European settlement in America. Moreover, the well-being of people in outlying areas tends to vary positively, not negatively, with the strength of connections to larger centers. Likewise, local solidarity, as expressed through collective mobilization to solve local problems, tends to increase with access to outside resources, not to decrease. A transformation might have occurred in the history of the community, but the transformation was well-advanced by the time communities were being formed by European migrants to North America. The transformation theory gives a plausible interpretation of some monumental changes years ago, but it is less useful for understanding trends and problems in modern communities.

The essential elements of the community were as problematic two centuries ago in North America as they are today, when compared to the ideal type of the ancient agrarian village. Territorial boundaries rarely have been fixed. The key point in understanding the territorial element of the community, however, is that the community has a geographic location, not that the boundaries of that location are fixed and sharply drawn. Similarly, the local society throughout modern history has been tied to the larger society through diverse channels. The local manifestations of society, nonetheless, are local. There is an unfortunate tendency in the community literature to draw a sharp distinction between the local and the extra-local. Most of the important social phenomena in a community are both local and extra-local, and local importance of a community characteristic often increases with the extent of its extra-local significance. Similarly, the observation that the community arena contains a turbulent field of self-seeking special interest games could have been made about American towns in the 1700s as well as today. In the midst of the turbulence now, as then, community emerges in the local society when the latent bond of common interest in the place—the shared investment in the common field of existential experience—draws people together and enables them to express common sentiments through joint action.

Community sociology needs a conception of the community relevant to the social conditions of the Western world of the past two or three centuries. What the sociology of community expresses mainly is a conception of community relevant to the Middle Ages and a lament that community thus conceived is being destroyed by long-distance communications, multi-site organizations, rationality of culture, and other modern trends. What is needed is a conception of community that recognizes its complexity. The community is an arena of both turbulence and cohesion, of order and disarray, of self-seeking and community-oriented interaction; and it manifests its dualities simultaneously. It should be studied for what it is and on its own grounds—not as an ideal type of an old form of social life, but as a dynamic and changing field of interacting forces.

Contrary to what is assumed in attempts to apply the transformation model today, a rural location can be a serious drag on community development. The transformation of society might be a reason for this, but that, as argued above, is old news. Rural location has been an impediment for many years to the realization of community in local settlements. As Durkheim (1933) explains, solidarity in the modern world requires moral (or dynamic) density, and moral density is low when material (or physical) density is low. Today that means rural areas have trouble supporting community.

In rural areas of modern society, the territory of the community typically is very large, contrary to the common observation that rural means a small place. Residents of rural areas often travel over a large territory to meet their daily needs. As Amos Hawley (1950:150) comments, the community can be defined ecologically by the territory within which the population meets its daily needs. The rural community territory tends to be so large, in fact, that it limits the strength of ties among the associations through which various needs are met. Further, many of these associations of rural people are located physically in distant urban centers, and residents of a given rural area often have direct personal involvements in several different centers. Consequently, rural residents tend to meet few of their daily needs together in the rural territory they share. This tendency could be a major long-time contributor to what only recently has come to be recognized as a serious barrier to the development of community in rural areas. A major problem of the rural community, therefore, is the lack of sufficient material density (to use Durkheim's terms) to support the level of moral or dynamic density needed for organic solidarity in modern times.

Another way of expressing this problem is with the idea of the "strength of weak ties," an idea applied in this study. Structural stability, according to Mark Granovetter (1973), depends on weak ties (i.e., on formal and transitory contacts among relative strangers) to bind strong ties (i.e., intimate and continuing relations among family members and friends) into larger structures. Otherwise, says Granovetter, "strong ties, breeding local cohesion, lead to overall fragmentation" (1973:1378). This is to say the strong ties in segments of a community can disrupt the whole of the community. Applying this notion to the rural setting, one finds evidence of a deficiency. Rural areas have plenty of strong ties, probably about the same number per capita as in urban areas, but they have few weak ties. The weak ties for residents of rural areas tend to be in contacts outside the rural area—in the larger rural–urban territory where rural people meet their daily needs. Thus, if this is correct, the shortage of weak ties in rural areas can retard the development of community.

Essays in critical theory point to another potential barrier to community development in rural areas or, from the perspective taken by Manuel Castells in *The Urban Question* (1977), another interpretation of the same situation as discussed from an ecological perspective. Using Marxian concepts, one can argue that urban-based capitalists organize and manipulate hinterland "peripheries" to assure maximum flow of profits on their investments to the centers where they extract and accumulate the profits. This entails assigning particular specialized uses to places, thus enforcing stratification among places. It also entails dependency, uneven development, and the instability that results from lack of diversity in a local economy. According to many discussions from the critical perspective, capitalist development in rural areas offers little promise of either rural economic development or of rural community development. Instead, development is said to be of benefit to the urban-based capitalists and to the rural elite who, in collaboration with the urban elite and government agencies, maintain rural peripheries in a state of dependent underdevelopment to assure ready access to resources.

From either of these perspectives, there can be little doubt that rural areas face serious problems of community. In recent years, for example, findings have challenged the earlier assumption that rural areas tend to have relatively low rates of such social problems as suicide and homicide. In fact, both of these rates (though not the rates of most violent crimes) tend to increase with the extent of rural settlement of local population when other important predictors are controlled (Wilkinson, 1984b). While much work needs to be done to specify the empirical connections between these rates and the extent of community in a local population, a logical connection can be drawn by applying Granovetter's concepts. Both suicide and homicide as specific events point to problems of disruption in strong ties—suicide because isolation from intimate contacts is a key etiological factor and homicide because victims and offenders usually are not strangers to one another. Thus, disruptions in strong ties could result from the shortage of weak ties in rural areas; and the disruptions in strong ties in turn could contribute to the tendency for suicide and homicide rates to increase with ruralness. Isolation thus threatens well-being in predominantly rural communities.

When the barriers to community interaction are reduced in either rural or urban settings, the quality of life tends to increase. This is seen in material changes but also in changes in the warmth and mutual regardingness of local social interaction. In rural areas, the principal barriers to community interaction are deficiencies in resources for meeting needs and inadequate social infrastructure of services, associations, and channels for collective action.

As rural sociology is an applied enterprise, many students of the rural community are interested in promoting rural community development as well as in understanding it. An agenda for research on rural communities, therefore, can contribute to an agenda for policy. This study assumes that an important item on either agenda should be to examine the concept of community itself for cues as to how the phenomenon it represents emerges and develops. A parallel task is to understand the meaning of "rural" in modern society and the problems this adjective implies for community interaction. These basic issues for theory and research have direct implications for practice and policy. Community, rural well-being, and community development are, in the first instance, objects in need of sociological investigation; but they also relate to normative issues of continuing importance in society. A goal of the study, therefore, is to understand the community and its contribution to rural well-being so that this contribution can be encouraged in practice.

The following chapters elaborate this perspective. Using an interactional theory of community and social well-being, the objective is to identify challenges to and prospects for the community in rural America. The first chapter outlines the interactional conception of the community. The second chapter examines the properties associated with rural location that affect the community. These chapters draw insights from theory and research in the sociological literature, and they address major conceptual issues about community and about rural life, respectively, using the interactional concepts. The third chapter presents the interactional concept of social well-being, relates that concept to the notion of community interaction, and explores the effects of rural location on the specific community interactions that influence well-being. The fourth chapter then analyzes the purposive development of community as a strategy to enhance social well-being in rural America. This chapter reviews the principal components of the development of community as a process and comments on actions that would encourage and protect this process in rural areas. The concluding chapter (Chapter 5) gathers together the several threads of the analysis, examines policy efforts to promote well-being in rural areas, and suggests ways rural sociology can support these efforts through research on the community.

INDIANA UNIVERSITY

Chapter 1

Pgs 54-60

Chapter 3

Pgs 113-115

1

The Community: An Interactional Approach

What is a community? Sociological definitions emphasize inter-personal bonds such as a shared territory, a common life, collective actions, and mutual identity. The essential ingredient is social interaction. Social interaction delineates a territory as the community locale; it provides the associations that comprise the local society; it gives structure and direction to processes of collective action; and it is the source of community identity. In sociological definitions of the community (Hillery, 1955) and in actual uses of this term in ordinary language and thought (Plant, 1974), one element stands out: the substance of community is social interaction.

An interactional theory of the community (see Kaufman, 1959, 1985; Kaufman and Wilkinson, 1967; Wilkinson, 1970b, 1986b) examines this intrinsic and indispensable property of the community and seeks to understand its relationships, as a constant, to changing community attributes. That also is what this study attempts. The setting is rural America, a milieu of rapid change in spatial, economic, and social organization. The study searches for evidence of community in this turbulent setting, asking whether the community is lost, saved, or liberated (see Wellman, 1979) in it.

The first step, and the task of this chapter, is to spell out the assumptions of the interactional conception of the community. Any theory of community must face certain conceptual issues,

including questions about the nature of the elemental bond of
community, the significance of place in community interaction,
and the survival of community in modern mass societies. A
review of these issues can help to distinguish the interactional
theory from others and to pose critical questions for analysis of
the community in rural America.

COMMUNITY: THE ELEMENTAL BOND

From the perspective of this study, the elemental bond occurs
in social interactions, specifically in interactions that embody and
express mutual interests in the common life of a local population.
Insights from the works of George Herbert Mead and Ferdinand
Toennies specify the nature of this bond in interpersonal transac-
tions. After considering the origins of community at this level,
the analysis moves to other levels where community interaction
is organized into locality-oriented processes and structures.

Social interaction, according to Mead (1934), is a process of
mutual "minding." People use their minds to understand the
meanings and intentions of the acts of others. In minding one
another, people send meanings back and forth, with the help of
symbols. Each actor, to understand the other, must take the point
of view of the other for interpreting the symbols. Thus, the actors
relate not only to one another's behaviors but to one another's
mind as well. The process builds a social bond of shared meaning,
and that bond becomes a fundamental part of the individual's
social being. Mead calls this bond of mutual meaning in social
interaction the "self."

The self arises in interactions with specific others and expands
in contact with what Mead calls the "generalized other," or
community. The community in Mead's work is the continuing
social process in which people are engaged. In this process people
form bonds with specific others but also with groups and with
"others in general." The interaction process is already there,
says Mead, with the individual in it, before the individual
becomes aware of self. Self-awareness is a recognition of the role

the individual plays in social interaction. This awareness arises as one individual takes the perspectives of others, including the perspective of the generalized other or community, to delineate and characterize one's own social being. The self, therefore, connects the individual and society. This elemental social bond consists of shared meanings among participants in processes of social interaction.

The interaction processes that produce this bond affect subsequent social behaviors in important ways. The most direct way, according to Mead's social psychological theory, is by affecting the volition or will of the individual. People act purposively in response to their concepts of connections among themselves. That is, they engage in willful, volitional behavior as they interact. This direct effect, of course, also is the starting place for the oldest and in many ways the most influential sociological theory of the community. Most sociological theories of community start with the work of Toennies (1957), who distinguishes two types of volition—the natural will and the rational will.

These types of volition or will, says Toennies, occur in social interaction and influence the social behavior of the individual and the structure of society. The natural will (*Wesenwille*) is impulsive; it simply moves the individual to act and does not involve deliberation or calculation. The rational will (*Kurwille*) on the other hand, is deliberative and calculating. It connects means to ends and recognizes the necessity to suppress impulses to attain goals. In elaborating a sociological theory from these concepts, Toennies examines various human associations, noting that in all empirical relationships the type of will fluctuates, being now natural and then rational, and so forth. As ideal or constructed types, *Gemeinschaft* refers to associations in which natural will predominates and *Gesellschaft* applies to associations conditioned fundamentally by the rational will. Neither type, however, refers to an actual group. Instead, *Gemeinschaft* and *Gesellschaft* refer to different forms of association that occur in all groups.

Herman Schmalenbach (1961), in a most perceptive essay, draws out the essence of Toennies' distinction between these forms of association and suggests that a third category is needed to complete the typology and to avoid some of the confusion that has resulted from use and misuse of Toennies' concepts, especially of *Gemeinschaft*. Community, says Schmalenbach, is a natural state of being-in-relationship to others. It is natural because the formative conditions of this state ordinarily are unconscious. Community simply exists in the fact that people have multiple and natural relationships with one another and these, taken as a whole, make up a common life. When community as a fact of living together is experienced, it is experienced as pre-existing, and not in and of itself as a sentiment or emotion about social relations, although, of course, it can involve emotions about other people. Community, says Schmalenbach, is something taken for granted, something self-evident in one's social behavior. Recognition of community can arouse feeling, but community itself simply refers to the fact that one naturally is connected to other people.

When this fact is recognized and responded to emotionally and the emotion is shared in interaction, a state that is different from community occurs, according to Schmalenbach. This new state is not *Gesellschaft*, because it is emotional and not rational in its basis. It can be called communion (a loose translation of the German word *Bund*). In Schmalenbach's words, communion arises "in the cognitive recognition of feeling" (1961:336) and expresses "recognition of a mutual sense of belonging." Communion, therefore, celebrates community.

Community, seen in this light, is natural and ubiquitous, and it occurs in interactions where it is interwoven with other social relationships. It is natural in that it is "real," not "nominal" (Zimmerman, 1938:653); and it is not contrived. This is to say the social interaction is authentic, not that it follows subsocial or biotic principles of organization as claimed by some human ecologists. It is natural because people, by the nature of being human, engage in social relationships with others on a continuing basis and they derive their social being and identities from social interaction. Community, likewise, is ubiquitous by virtue of the fact that all people engage in it almost all of the time, whether or not they recognize that fact. From the natural flow of the interaction processes, community emerges, and the fact of its existence, whether or not celebrated in communion, affects the social processes that follow its emergence. Community, therefore, is a natural disposition among people who interact with one another on various matters that comprise a common life.

It is instructive that neither Toennies nor Mead restricts community to relationships based only on positive sentiments. In fact, sentiment as such is not the stuff of community in either of their concepts. Community simply depends on people interacting with one another, and people interact in all kinds of ways. Even as they are engaged in the most calculating of exchanges, such as those Toennies calls *Gesellschaft*, they engage simultaneously in *Gemeinschaft*. This is true because, as Mead says, all social interaction involves shared meaning and exchange of perspectives. Without these there could be no rational exchange. Moreover, community entails squabbles and fights as well as cooperation and affectionate touches. Indeed, community implies all types of relations that are natural among people, and if interaction is suppressed, community is limited. The unsuppressed flow of human interaction, regulated naturally by the requirements of interaction itself (e.g., by the necessity to give and receive symbolic messages and to take the perspective of the other in understanding self and others), is the elemental stuff of which community is made.

To be sure, as well, neither Toennies nor Mead would restrict community to the local community. For Toennies, *Gemeinschaft* (community) rather than *Gemeinde* (local community) signifies the natural bond. For Mead, the community is the general social process within which specific interactions are nested. Neither theorist specifies a territorial bond. Their ideas, nonetheless, can be used to study the elemental bond of community within the local community, although, of course, to use their ideas for this purpose is to broach a highly controversial issue in recent literature on the sociology of community, that issue being the connection between community and locality.

TERRITORY

Sociological definitions of the community have usually emphasized a given territory, and the approach of this study accepts local territory as a necessary element of the community. As Thomas Bender observes: "The most common sociological definitions used today tend to focus on a community as an aggregate of people who share a common interest in a particular locality. Territorially based social organization and social activity thus define a community" (1978:5).

E. T. Hiller (1941), in a classic essay, concludes that the community, as an abstract concept, meets all of the requirements of being a social group; but he adds a fifth element by which the community is differentiated from other groups, namely, "a habitat, locality or area." Talcott Parsons (1960:250) discusses the community as "that aspect of the structure of social systems which is referable to the territorial location of persons (i.e., human individuals as organisms) and their activities." In elaborating this tentative definition (1960:250-79), he argues that some elements of the social system, as he defines it (1951), occur in concrete form in specific territories. In summarizing his view of the "communicative aspect of the social system," for example, he says, "The upshot of this discussion of communication is to make it clear that not only must *activities* of members of a social system be spatially located, and hence their distribution patterned, but the physical aspects of the processes of interaction *between* social units much be definitely patterned (emphasis *sic*)."

The idea that physical aspects of social interaction are patterned is developed most fully, of course, in human ecology, notably by Amos Hawley, who says, "Formally defined, community refers to the structure of relationships through which a localized population provides its daily requirements. . . . It is, in fact, the least reducible universe within which ecological phenomena may be adequately observed. . . . The community, then, is the basic unit of ecological investigation" (1950:180).

Indeed, as Rene Konig (1968:15) says, the German word *Gemeinschaft* (community) referred originally to common lands of the community, and only later did this word come to refer more broadly to social aspects of a common life.

As noted by Harold Kaufman (1959, 1985), the interactional definition of community builds upon this conventional approach to community as place. The analysis begins with place and people and then moves quickly to consider social interactions. The key interactions are those that express "locality-orientation" (Wilkinson, 1970a). Place, in this conception is an essential element of the community.

The relationship between community and locality, however, has become a controversial issue in the sociology of community, and objections to the territorial element must be considered carefully before using the interactional approach to examine the community in rural America.

Perhaps the most widely endorsed argument against retaining the territorial element is that contacts of people outside the immediate place of residence have become commonplace. Transportation, communications, large-scale organizations and other mechanisms now link people to multiple localities. Perhaps in the past, at least in some localities, the local territory contained a more or less complete and distinctive community; but today, according to those who make this objection (e.g., Bender, 1978; Gusfield, 1975), a territory-free concept of community should be preferred. A territory-free concept would suggest that people could participate simultaneously in many different communities.

Bender (1978) develops this thesis in an impressive historical analysis of the community in America. In addition to his analysis of the myth of community in small towns, which is addressed in another chapter of this study, his comments on the nature of the community are insightful. Community takes many structural forms, he says, but in any context it consists of "a network of social relations marked by mutuality and emotional bonds"

(1978:7). Granting the importance of mutuality and emotional bonds, the local community, he says, is only one setting for these relations. He observes: "Territorially based interaction represents only one pattern of community, a pattern that becomes less and less evident over the course of American history" (1978:6). From Bender's perspective, communities should be sought, not in particular places but in intimate networks wherever these might occur.

Barry Wellman (1979) and Wellman and Barry Leighton (1979) develop a similar perspective in discussing what they call "The Community Question," which is a question about the survival of primary ties in modern society, specifically about "how large-scale divisions of labor in social systems affect the organization and content of interpersonal ties" (Wellman and Leighton, 1979:365). This question need not refer, Wellman says, to localities; instead sociologists should "search for functioning primary ties, wherever located and however solidary" (1979:1202). In fact, Wellman maintains, ties outside the locality (by which he means the neighborhood) can free people so that "their ties are not encapsulated in 'decoupled' little worlds" (1979:1227). Drawing on Melvin Webber's (1964) essay on "community without propinquity," they argue that ramified networks can provide an escape from the bondage of the local territory.

Mobility certainly increases the number of outside contacts. One critic of the territorial definition of community, Jacqueline Scherer (1972), argues that physical mobility, at least for the middle and upper classes, has put an end to "place chains." Moreover, she says, "psychological mobility," facilitated by mass communications, has reduced the tie of locality for all classes. Mobility means choice as to associations and place of residence; consequently, from this viewpoint, where one resides no longer indicates a "uniting of social forms" to a place (1972:19).

A somewhat different challenge to the idea of community as locality is posed by Don Martindale (1963), who argues that the territory of community has expanded to encompass the nation as a whole, leaving local communities to wither. He writes "The modern city is losing its external and internal structure. Internally it is in a state of decay. The new community represented by the nation everywhere grows at its expense" (1963:166). This theme is similar to Edward Shils' (1972:299-47) defense of the "mass society," which he sees not as a sign of the demise of local well-being but as evidence of integration of the population into the central value and institutional systems of society. The mass society is a welfare society promoting egalitarian ideals. It is a form of community to be achieved as a societal goal, and not something to be resisted as a sign of the decay of community. As mass society, community transcends the local society.

A number of writers also question the territorial element in community definition on the grounds that the emphasis on this element often expresses an anti-urban bias. The idea of the community as a territorial settlement, says Joseph Gusfield (1975:31), "has its roots in the tendency to identify the local, small territorial unit with communal relationships and the large urban and regional units with societal concepts." Rejecting this tendency, which is found in classical essays on the city by Louis Wirth (1938) and Georg Simmel (1950) and in rural sociology, as pointed out by Bruno Benvenuti et al. (1975) and Peter Saunders et al. (1978), Joseph Gusfield also calls for the abandonment of the territorial concept in favor of studying the community as a social phenomenon only.

An additional question about the territorial community is in the observation (e.g., by Castells, 1977; Bell and Newby, 1972; Molotch, 1976; Wellman, 1979) that solidarity on a locality basis suppresses the expression of real interests of classes other than the local elite. By this argument, community mobilization tends to be class action, and localism as an ideology serves only the interest of those in the community who control key resources such as land and housing. As Stephen Lukes (1974) notes, the power of the dominant class can extend even to shaping the wants and wishes of others. Thus, class hegemony can create a false appearance of community cohesion (see Bridger, 1988:78-9).

Taken together, these objections seem to present a formidable threat to the territorial concept of the community. The argument behind that threat, however, is flawed in several ways and each major criticism can be countered with good reasons for continuing to emphasize *local* social interaction in the sociology of the community.

The most obvious flaw is in rejecting the simple fact that most people, past and present, live and move and have most of their being in everyday life in local settlements. This is true even though extensive contacts occur among people in different settlements and even though much of the social life in any settlement has little to do with the locality. Amos Hawley, explaining why collective life is universal, gives a succinct and compelling answer: "It is simply that organisms either live together or they don't live" (1950:177). People live together in localities. Moreover, we cannot dismiss the fact that people in local settlements continue to interact with one another daily in the process of conducting various aspects of their lives. Jessie Bernard expresses this point as follows:

At the local community level there is confrontation, visual if not tactile, emotional if not intellectual. People still live next door to others, they eat, sleep, love, hate, avoid, or seek one another in a given locale. Whether or not they have much to do with their neighbors, they use the same grocery store or supermarket, attend the same movie houses, and patronize the same beauty parlors or barber shops. Owners or renters, they depend on the same community services such as, humble as they may be, garbage collection, street cleaning, and police protection. However emancipated from spatial barriers and however independent of locale the elite may be, it is still on the community scene that for most human beings interaction takes place. These phenomena cannot be just read out of the discipline (1973:187).

If the essence of community is a natural process of social interaction, as assumed here, there is little doubt that community can occur in local settlements where people interact with one another daily. The local territory, therefore, is a logical place to begin the search for community, even if the study takes one beyond the locality as well.

A most important consideration in the decision to retain a territorial element for this study is the realization that the local settlement itself is a product of social interaction. While characteristics of the local ecology certainly can influence interaction, it is the social interaction that first delineates and then maintains the local ecology as a unit. This is to say that social interaction defines territory, and not the opposite. The borders, as one might call them, of a local territory are forever in flux, depending on the movements of people. The "built" features of local ecology, such as roads and buildings, give structure to some of the interactions that occur in a locality, but to recognize this is not to deny that these features are built by human beings in interaction with one another and that interactions can change the built environment in the future. Thus, the study of how interaction processes shape and are shaped by local territory is an appropriate focus for the sociology of community.

The idea that interaction defines territory agrees, of course, with the suggestion by network theorists that sociologists should plot the social networks among people to see where in fact they occur. Community interaction rarely is restrained by fixed locality borders. One could argue that what the local settlement consists of socially is a network, and that this network delineates the locality. Paul Craven and Barry Wellman (1973) make such an argument about cities, calling them "networks of networks." Wellman and Leighton (1979) point out that by going outside the neighborhood, urban residents can become part of a larger network in the metropolitan field. One can see in this point, contrary to Wellman and Leighton's view of the neighborhood as the locality, that the total locality—the metropolis in their analysis—is the local territory that results from social interaction.

Thus, rather than rejecting the territorial element, the interactional conception of the community supports the view that contacts among people define the local territory; and it argues, from a base in inductive logic, that characteristics of local settlements are important indicators (i.e., markers or products) of social interaction. With an inductive method, the community is something to be discovered, as are its elements and characteristics (see Hillery, 1968). Discovery requires detailed study of the social life of people. The study begins where the student thinks community might be located—in a territory where people live and act together. From this point of entry, one traces the actions and connections among people, discovering sometimes that interaction processes expand in space far beyond the point of departure of the study, but learning also in the usual case that community arises in territorially-based relationships within the locality.

On the matter of mobility and freedom from bondage to a fixed locality, a question might be raised as to whether residential mobility has increased or decreased over the past century or so (Fischer, 1977:191). There is little doubt that various developments in contact technology, especially in long-distance communication (see Hawley, 1978), have increased the frequency of interactions among people in different localities. Whether this means that the historical relationship between community and place has been weakened, however, remains an empirical question. Claude Fischer (1977:192) agrees that choice has increased, but rejects the idea that attachment to particular places has declined as a result. What has declined, he says, is constraint or involuntary limitation to a place. Fewer people now are forced to stay in a place and fewer are forced to leave. People have more choices than in the past, and the result no doubt is a change in the local community but not necessarily a decline in the extent of community in the locality.

In addition, the argument that territoriality is class hegemony posing as community, while no doubt true in some cases (Bridger, 1988; Massey, 1980), generally underestimates the tendency for quiescence to become conflict (Gaventa, 1980) and the potential for conflict to encourage community development (Robinson, 1989). Quiescence changes into conflict when conditions permit a challenge to inequality. The reason this occurs is not because people are forced to give up a treasured state of peaceful subservience but because community—a powerful natural bond—demands that inequality be challenged. This bond exists even where its expression is suppressed and even where dominant and dominated groupings appear to be locked into a system of accommodation to inequality. Community is the natural force that breaks down such a system. Moreover, as recognized by critics of capitalist development in literature heralding the recent "rediscovery" of the locality (Bradley and Lowe, 1984), the local territory is where class and community dynamics are played out.

There is an unresolved empirical question as to the extent to which community, as discussed by Toennies and distinguished from communion, can exist except in local social interaction. This is an unsettled matter, notwithstanding the fact that people in modern society have important relationships outside the community. What Toennies describes as natural bonds among people who share a common life clearly can occur within the local community. Whether they occur in territory-free networks, however, is in question. A test would be to measure the extent to which the natural processes involved in Toennies' *Gemeinschaft* do in fact occur and persist among people who are not in face-to-face interaction or whose contacts are only occasional. From the standpoint of an interactional theory, *Gemeinschaft* is assumed to occur mainly (if not exclusively) in direct and continuing contacts among people who share a local territory.

In the extreme, there is no doubt that a *sense* of community can exist with little contact, but there is a question as to the extent to which community itself exists. The question to be asked would not be whether people feel a sense of community (or communion) with those contacted rarely or only indirectly. The question, following Toennies, would be whether the actual contacts among people, existing prior to the rise of a sense or sentiment of solidarity, are extensive enough to constitute community. It is a question, then, about social interaction.

The community—and precisely the local community or *Gemeinde*—is where, as Rene Konig says, "social life takes on the highest possible degree of tangibility" (1968:4). Community exists in social interaction and not in thoughts about relationships. With increasing abstraction from the daily experiences of people, it seems apparent that the potential for community recedes. The local territory, where social life is least abstract, is where the search for community must begin.

Willis Sutton and Jiri Kolaja (1960a:325) say that the characteristic particularly unique to the community as an interaction process is "the locality orientation of the action patterns." Locality orientation, which is indicated by the characteristics of actors, by the extent of local awareness of the actions, and by the goals of action and its recipients, is what defines the extent of "community-ness" of local action patterns. While the concept of locality/orientation has been used mainly as they use it—that is, to distinguish more or less organized episodes of "community action" from other processes in local populations (see Kaufman, 1959; Sutton and Kolaja, 1960b; Wilkinson, 1970a)—the idea of community-ness has implications for study of informal social interactions as well. All social interactions and all of the relationships they build can be said to vary in extent of community-ness.

The truism that everything happens somewhere gives, of course, a nominal base—but only a nominal base—of locality relevance to every social interaction. Above this base, variation in community-ness can be assessed according to (1) the extent of "community" or *Gemeinschaft* in the interaction, as discussed by Toennies (and as distinguished from communion), and (2) the extent to which characteristics of the locality, including place, people, and the associations they share, are salient in the shared meanings that arise in the interaction. The former of these refers to variation in "community," which as Toennies assumes is not restricted inherently to locality-oriented interaction. The latter refers to variation in the form of community that is of special concern to the interactional study of *the* community, which is to say the *local* community.

The locality gives the territorial setting for the interactional community to emerge, but "a common life" implies more than being together in space; and "locality-oriented" action is oriented to more than the shared territory. The locality is the starting place for analysis because it is the point or locus of empirical convergence of the multiple threads that make up a community; but it is only a starting place. Having located a point of departure, the analysis of community shifts from a focus on territory to a focus on the social life of the people whose behaviors give the territory its social meaning.

COMMUNITY AND SOCIETY

Most theories of the community in sociology concentrate not on the locality but on the local society. The local society is the organization of social institutions and associations in the social life of the local population. This organization is important because it is the smallest complete form of the larger abstraction we call "society" and, as such, it is the most accessible form of society for study. Theories of community typically examine society in the local setting where people experience it directly in their daily lives.

As a local society, the community is a social whole, though rarely is it a self-sufficient or exclusive one. It is a global unit, containing a comprehensive array of groups and other social relationships, but its members can belong simultaneously to other social units as well (Konig, 1968:23-25). The community in this sense has a full round of the ordinary activities of people and a full complement of the social structures through which a common life is organized. Moreover, the ideal type of the community as local society is an integrated unit; its parts interconnect with one another giving it wholeness and distinctiveness.

Of the comprehensive and integrated local society, R. M. MacIver writes, "The mark of a community is that one's life *may* (emphasis *sic*) be lived wholly within it" (MacIver and Page, 1949:9). His point is that the community covers and integrates all aspects of a common life, as distinguished, for example, from an association. He writes, "A community is a focus of social life, the common living of social beings; an association is an organization of social life, definitely established for the pursuit of one or more common interests. An association is partial; a community is integral" (MacIver, 1931:24).

Conrad Arensberg (1961:254) has a similar idea when he says the community, whether taken as an object of study itself or as a sample of society, must have the entire "table of organization" of society—"persons and roles and statuses, or the transmitted and learned awareness of them, for every kind of office of mankind that the culture knows." The local society need not be the "cradle to the grave arrangement" Robert Redfield (1955:4) describes in *The Little Community*, but its structure must be generalized and nothing important about society must be missing from it.

The idea of completeness of the local society should not be confused with the image of a settlement surrounded by walls holding its inhabitants in and keeping others out. One can shop or work or engage in various institutions outside the local society without altering the completeness of the social organization within the settlement. The important question is whether local social life itself includes the opportunities for shopping, work, or other activities people engage in regularly. The local society includes and interrelates all such activities.

Furthermore, the local society is an open society, existing as a "community among communities" (Redfield, 1955), and having extensive ties to other communities and to the larger society. It retains its distinctive focus as a complete and unified local entity even though people pass through its open structure, coming and going as they relate to smaller units, such as the family and neighborhood, and larger ones, such as the nation, at the same time they relate to the local society itself.

The idea of the community as local society is central to human ecological and social systems theories that have dominated the sociology of the community in the twentieth century. The early human ecologists, notably Robert Park, Ernest Burgess, and Roderick McKenzie (1925), rejected the idea that local settlements are organized spatially or functionally by social forces. Instead, taking principles from biological ecology, they attempted to explain community morphology—the development and form of its fundamental structures—through references to subsocial phenomena only. Hawley (1944), rejecting their distinction between the social and the subsocial (see Hawley, 1948:156), pointed out that while ecology is indeed the morphological study of community organization, biological principles give only a partial view of the structure of the human community. His book *Human Ecology: A Theory of Community Structure* (1950) establishes the modern focus of the field of human ecology in sociology (see Micklin, 1984). That focus is on the organization of *social* life in local territories.

In Hawley's framework, human behavior, including the capacity to produce culture, is "but a further manifestation of the tremendous potential for adjustment inherent in organic life" (1950:69); this potential is expressed collectively among humans, as among most organisms, through "ecological organization" (1950:178); and the community, he says, is the basic form of ecological organization (1950:180). He defines community simply as "the structure of relationships through which a localized population provides its daily requirements" (1950:180). That these relations are social—a term Hawley uses to refer to all interdependencies among people and not merely to those of nonbiotic origin (1948:156)—is expressed in his analysis of the essential elements of community structure. These elements include the corporate, symbiotic relations in the co-action of unlike forms and the categoric, commensalistic relations in the co-action of like forms: "The community is thus a symbiotic-commensalistic phenomenon" (1950:209). Numerous differences among communities can be predicted depending on how these elements are distributed and interconnected in particular cases (see Duncan and Reiss, 1956). While Hawley notes that the community is not the only form of ecological organization, he says, "It is in fact, the least reducible universe within which ecological phenomena may be adequately observed" (1950:180). Further, while his view of human ecology restricts it to a study of "the structural features of functional organization and how these change in response to changes in external conditions" (1950:180), and while critics might refer to Hawley's version of human ecology as "neoclassical capitalism writ in space" (Gilbert, 1982:623), his theory provides a broad framework of knowledge of community structure in which questions about cultural, psychological, interactional and other aspects of local social life might well be couched (Murdock and Sutton, 1974).

Similarly, the general concept of the community as a social system emphasizes the structure and integration of the local version of society. The basic idea of the community as system, in the words of Lowry Nelson et al., "is that it operates as a unit, and to do this, it has a system or structure of interrelated parts" (1960:2). Parsons, whose general theory of the social system (1951) has been applied at several levels of analysis of social organization, uses the concept of the community in two ways, namely (as mentioned above) as "that aspect of the structure of social systems which is referable to the territorial location of persons . . . and their activities" (1960:250) and as an integrative mechanism of the society as a whole, which he calls the "societal community" (1966:10-19). These usages, however, differ mainly in the level of abstraction. The community to Parsons is the manifestation of selected aspects of society in the local territory where people live. It includes, he says, "*persons acting in territorial locations*, and since the reference is to *social* relations, persons acting in relation *to other persons* in respect to the territorial locations of both parties" (emphasis *sic*) (1960:251). The elements of community structure in his analysis (i.e., the aspects of social systems that are referable to territory) are residential location, occupation and work premises, and jurisdiction, which refers to legitimate obligations imposed on categories of people (1960:258). These elements are linked, he says, by the communicative complex that coordinates behavior and provides order. This, he points out, is a social order based on normative institutions and rules and must, therefore, "in the nature of the case, have a territorial reference" (1960:278). The basic idea is that the community represents the grounding of certain aspects of society in real time and space—in the locations where and when people interact.

The object of attention of a social systems theory, be it either a theory of closed-systems or of open-systems (see Katz and Kahn, 1966), is *order*—order in the patterning and interrelationships of the various components of social organization. Well-known sociological analyses of the community as a social system by Charles Loomis and J. Allan Beegle (1957), George Hillery (1968), Frederick Bates and Lloyd Bacon (1972), Irwin Sanders (1966), Roland Warren (1978), and many others (see Poplin, 1979) take separate approaches to understanding repeated and structured interaction in the local population. They agree that interaction follows systemic patterns, and they agree, or at least they all imply, that the local society itself, insofar as it constitutes a community, is a social system—or, more properly, a local system of systems.

Warren's (1978) discussion of "The American Community as a Social System" is perhaps the best known and most complete conceptual analysis of the community from this perspective. He states the assumptions of the social system concept as follows:

A social system is a structural organization of the interaction of units which endures through time. It has both external and internal aspects relating the system to its environment and its units to each other. It can be distinguished from the surrounding environment, performing a function called boundary maintenance. It tends to maintain an equilibrium in the sense that it adapts to changes from outside the system in such a way as to minimize the impact of the change on the organizational structure and to regularize the subsequent relationships (1978:136).

Then, taking these assumptions as criteria, he asks a series of questions about American communities to determine the extent to which they display the defining characteristics of social systems.

His initial answer is that American communities, to varying degrees, do have systemic characteristics, although community subsystems tend to be tied more strongly to extracommunity systems than to one another. Defining the community system as "that combination of social units and systems which perform the major social functions having locality relevance" (1978:136), he concludes that trends in America, representing the continued unfolding of a "Great Change," are shifting the locus of systemic integration and equilibrium away from the community's horizontal (local) axis and onto its vertical (extra-local) axis.

Subsequently, in a new chapter in the third edition of his book, Warren (1978:408-22) draws a distinction between two general approaches to studying the community as a social system. One, based on Parsons' (1960) model, sees the community as a concrete collectivity, and the other, based on what he calls "the interaction field approach," sees the community "not as a collective entity but as the simple aggregate of the clustered interaction of people and organizations occupying a restricted geographic area, whose aggregate interaction, in both structure and function, demonstrates not chaos or randomness but large areas of systemic interconnections" (Warren, 1978:409). The former, a "concrete collectivity" approach, emphasizes the pervasive and continuing organization of the local society as a whole, and the latter, an "interaction field" approach, emphasizes the community as an arena within which different degrees of interaction take place among individuals and organizations. Given Warren's view of the declining importance of place as a basis of social organization and the increasing significance of "macrosystem" features in organizing various local activities, he argues that this newer, interactional paradigm has much more to offer for understanding the American community than does the concept of the community as a concrete collectivity.

Granting the criteria Warren uses to ask about whether the social system concept applies to the American community, one must conclude from the evolution of his argument across the three editions of *The Community in America* that in his view the idea of a community system has little utility today, although the concept of community as an interaction field has much utility. As he notes (1978:412-13), most of the major developments in community theory over recent decades represent more or less direct challenges to the social system concept. The challenges, namely, the interactional approach of Harold Kaufman and associates, the search for community in organizations and other affiliations rather than in the locality, and the space-free concepts in analysis of urban networks, raise questions not only about the idea of the community system as a concrete collectivity, as Warren suggests, but also about the utility of the social system concept in any approach to the community. These theories emphasize the dynamic, emergent aspects of community life, while the system concept continues to focus mainly on tendencies toward stability and forces that resist change.

A logical response is to shift the emphasis from the system to the field. As Harry Turney-High (1968) argues, social life in any setting has both system (which he attributes to gravity) and turbulence, and both of these should be studied to understand community. A question can be raised, however, as to whether it is useful to pose the initial questions in research and to develop the initial methods with one of these poles in mind when the other pole apparently is dominant in the field to be studied. What has been developing in community theory is not a new approach to studying the community *system* but a new approach to studying the *community*, an approach that sees the community mainly as a field of social interaction rather than as a social system.

New developments also question the usefulness of viewing the human community as a human ecological system, notwithstanding the continuing importance of ecological factors in community interaction. While people live in collective settlements and meet most needs through interactions in small local territories, they do so through adaptive structures that extend far beyond the local space and are organized at national, regional, and world levels. The "Great Change" to which Warren attributes the shift from the concrete collectivity to the field approach in theories of community also contains forces that challenge the idea of the community as an integral unit in human ecology. These include, in particular, developments in transportation and long-distance communications that integrate the separate sectors of local economies into larger economic systems. While these developments appear to be reducing the dependency of small settlements on nearby centers (Hawley, 1978; Johansen and Fuguitt, 1984) by connecting the latter instead directly to national and international centers of decision-making in large firms, the ties they support are between specific sectors of the community and firms in the larger society and not between the community as a whole and the larger society. Consequently, writing from a critical viewpoint, Richard Walker (1978) observes a tendency for economic development in smaller centers to be highly concentrated, often occurring only in a single sector. This can result in an ecological or adaptive vulnerability for the local community as a whole, even though development in the single sector might be of some benefit to the local population. Changes in the larger economy that depress a particular employment sector, for example, could leave the community with no alternative sources of employment. The kind of diversified development that would support a flexible, adaptive organization often occurs not in local areas but in the larger society to which parts of the community are linked.

Given these observations, one must ask: What is left to be said about the community in America? It has a local ecology, but by and large the distinctiveness of local ecologies is thought by many to be a thing of the past. It has institutions and associations, but by and large these are described as elements of the larger society represented on the local scene. There are values and rules of behavior, but these are rooted more in national culture or in individual and family experiences than in local structure. There are networks and organizations, but these tend to expand beyond the locality. It is not hard to see how leading students of the community would turn away from the local society or how the public quest for community would look for opportunities for this phenomenon to emerge in other settings. It also is not surprising that sociological research on the local community would almost disappear. This is not surprising, that is, until the study of the community turns or, more precisely, until it *returns* to the topic of social interaction. In interaction, the community persists as a distinctive, centering element of local social life in America.

COMMUNITY INTERACTION

The study of social interaction continues to be a fruitful area of inquiry in the sociology of the community. If local ecology and local society no longer denote a holistic unit, community interaction is another matter. People who live together tend to interact with one another whether or not they participate in extra-local structures as well. Moreover, their interactions can form a community field even if the community is not an ecological or social system. With a focus on social interaction, the sociology of the community continues to address important issues about completeness and integration of social life.

From the interactional perspective, a community is a dynamic field rather than a system. As the terms field and system have been used in the behavioral and social sciences (see Mey, 1972; Yinger, 1965), both refer to a holistic structure among interacting units. Both terms, therefore, refer to an important aspect of the conventional meaning of the community, namely, the quality of being a complete and integrated whole. The main difference is that with the field concept, attention is directed more to the dynamic processes that create and alter community structure than to the effects of structure on social processes. While a social system struggles to maintain its boundaries and to reinforce its existing order of internal relationships, a field is an unbounded whole with a constantly changing structure (Wilkinson, 1970b:313-14). Social interaction is the dynamic, creative force that redefines and articulates the relationships among actors that comprise the structure of the community field. System reifies the community as an organic whole, but field simply describes the community as a process of human interaction.

As this approach has been outlined by Kaufman (1959, 1985), the community field is but one of the fields of interaction in a local population. Other fields are distinguished from the community field and from one another by the interests that the actors pursue in interaction. Following MacIver and Page (1949:24), interests are the objects of action. They are the stimuli or goals that give direction to a social process. Within a population, research can identify several fields of interaction that pursue or express particular interests. Within each field, an analysis can describe the activities and associations of the actors as they pursue that particular interest. Thus, a number of more or less distinct social fields make up the community.

The community field, along with other fields, has actors, associations (both organized and unorganized), and activities directed toward certain interests, but in the community field, unlike the others, the interests are generalized and intrinsic; they are not specialized or instrumental. The community field cuts across organized groups and across other interaction fields in a local population. It abstracts and combines the locality-relevant aspects of the special interest fields, and integrates the other fields into a generalized whole. It does this by creating and maintaining linkages among fields that otherwise are directed toward more limited interests. As this community field arises out of the various special interest fields in a locality, it in turn influences those special interest fields and asserts the community interest in the various spheres of local social activity.

Why does the community field arise? This is a key question for theory and research. Warren, discussing the community as a turbulent arena where outside actors and special interest groups encounter one another, observes that the heart of community theory is in trying to understand "how the whole thing hangs together, even though there is often little collectivity orientation and even though many of the parts are organizationally structured as integral parts of systems whose control mechanisms may be located hundreds or thousands of miles away" (1978:411). From the interactional perspective, the answer to Warren's question is found in the tendency for people who live together to interact with one another on place-relevant matters irrespective of the fact that they are involved simultaneously in multiple special interest fields, some of which connect them to systems outside the locality. As noted earlier, interaction among community residents is a form of *Gemeinschaft*, which itself is a structure-building force. This elemental bond of community exists because people in social interaction are never simply the parties to a contractual exchange or the impersonal performers of normatively assigned roles. The special form of *Gemeinschaft* among people who live together has a locality orientation, and this contributes to the emergence of a community field by instituting a generalized bond—one that cuts across and links special interest activities within the local territory. Moreover, this generalized locality-oriented bond can be recognized and celebrated by the participants as "communion" (Schmalenbach, 1961), and under certain conditions, to be discussed later, this bond can become an object as well as a means of purposive collective action among local residents (see Wilkinson, 1972). The short answer to why the community "hangs together" is that a community field tends to occur where people live together and interact on matters concerning their common interest in the locality.

The study of community interaction in the local society has identified episodes, events, and processes called community actions (see Wilkinson, 1970a). These are collective behaviors of local residents that address explicitly local issues, issues that are, in Sutton and Kolaja's terms, "derived from the common use of the particular area" (1960a:326). Community actions are collective actions that occur intermittently, if at all (see Tilly, 1973), when a common interest in place-relevant matters is aroused.

Measures of the frequency, interconnection, and other characteristics of community actions are useful for describing the most
highly visible manifestations of community in a locality.
The field of locality-oriented social interaction, however, is not
restricted to organized projects. Community actions as highly
visible projects draw from and express a broad bond of community that exists also in the everyday life of a local population. The
potential for this pervasive bond to exist rests in part on the
tendency for *Gemeinschaft* to occur in all interpersonal relationships, irrespective of the content of the interaction in the relationship. *Gemeinschaft* tends to occur even if *Gesellschaft* dominates
the relationship. Warren makes this point in musing, "Where Has
All the Gemeinschaft Gone?" The answer, he says, is that it is
very much still here and can be seen "in the extensive informal
helping networks, in the ad hoc development of coalitions for
local purposes, in the strength of sociometric ties, in the meaningful associations within a religious group, an ethnic group, or
other group with common bonds of interest, and in the personal
bonds of affection and sentiment that spring up among people in
interaction in even the most formal settings" (1978:419). So long
as people interact, community in this sense will persist and give
rise to collective identity and action in the locality.

The community field, however, as Kaufman (1959:10) insists,
is no all-inclusive "Mother Hubbard." It does not contain all
of the social relationships in a local population. The
Gemeinschaftlich quality of all social interaction, much of which
occurs in the locality, gives only a general basis for the emergence
of the interactional community in the locality, just as it gives a
general basis for what Bender (1978), Gusfield (1975), and others
see as the potential for community to arise in nonlocal settings.
Community action as a special case of collective action draws
from a special case of *Gemeinschaft*. In the general case, *Gemeinschaft* arises because people engage naturally in social interaction,
and social interaction demands and assures that they form a
commonality as they share meanings through symbolic communication. They are bound together naturally in this most human

and communal of processes whatever the content of the meaning they share and whatever they might think or feel about one another. In community action, as defined from the interactional perspective (Wilkinson, 1970a), the interacting parties form a *Gemeinschaft* that gives special content and meaning to their interaction. The special quality in this form of *Gemeinschaft* is locality orientation. Each actor has a real interest in the *local* aspects of local social life. This interest, which local residents have in common whether or not they experience it consciously, is pursued in social interaction and thus is shared. This particular shared interest that arises in social interaction—the shared interest in things local—gives the elemental bond of the interactional community. It is distinguished from other bonds of *Gemeinschaft* by its locality orientation.

An understanding of the interactional community therefore makes use of Toennies' concept of *Gemeinschaft* but specifies a more restricted focus than the general type of social bond *Gemeinschaft* often implies. This more specific concept does not include all of *Gemeinschaft* that one might find in a society or even all that one might find in the social life of a local population. It is a bond that emerges specifically in local social interaction as common interests in local aspects of social life become shared interests. Thus the locality is a most important consideration in studying the interactional community although the territory itself is not the focus of inquiry.

DEVELOPMENT OF THE COMMUNITY

While the potential for community interaction exists in any human settlement, the extent of development of the community field in fact is highly variable from locality to locality and from time to time in given localities. This variation results from factors that suppress and restrict social interaction. Obviously, in the absence of social interaction there would be no interactional community; but some interaction occurs wherever people live together. The principal constraints to the development of community in a local population, therefore, are barriers to the specific kinds of interaction that make up a community field. These barriers are emphasized in the argument that the local community has lost its significance in the modern age in favor of ties that do not refer to specific territory. From the interactional perspective, however, such an argument ignores the fact that people still live and interact with one another in local settlements. Thus the development of territory-free ties does not, in and of itself, alter the fact that people have territory-based contacts as well. Attachments to structures other than the community are barriers to community development only if they constrain community interaction. In general, from the interactional perspective, the principal constraints to the development of community are factors that interfere with the particular kind of *Gemeinschaft* that is locality relevant. These factors contribute to variation in the extent of emergence of the community field in local settlements by affecting the extent to which the local territory can support a local society. Rural and urban characteristics of the local society are important factors to be investigated in this light.

2

The Rural–Urban Variable in Community Research

The rural–urban variable appears to be making something of a comeback in the sociology of the community. Prior to the 1960s, the idea of a rural-to-urban transition was at the center of community theory, and innumerable case studies sought to document degrees and consequences of this transition in communities at various points along a rural–urban continuum. But in the 1960s and 1970s this approach fell into disrepute and the rural–urban variable fell into disuse. Sociologists—including rural sociologists—turned to other variables in the quantitative studies that were beginning to dominate the field. Remarkably, community studies fell out of favor at about the same time. The recent rebirth of interest in the rural–urban variable coincides with a revival of interest in the community, or at least in the locality. This chapter traces the checkered history of community research in rural sociology, examines the key issues that have led to shifts in emphasis in this history, and uses these as background for a new look at the connection between rural life and community in the modern world. Cast in the light of an interactional perspective, both the community and the rural–urban variable still have much to offer rural sociology.

COMMUNITY STUDIES

Literally from the time of its origins around the turn of the twentieth century, American sociology as a field of empirical research has relied heavily on studies of small communities. These have given insights into patterns of everyday social life and processes of social change. The earliest studies of rural communities by sociologists were conducted by students of Franklin H. Giddings of Columbia University, who viewed the community as a natural laboratory for inductive research on social institutions and change (Hollingshead, 1948:138). The early studies (e.g., Sims, 1912; Williams, 1906) described town and country life in detail in small village-centered settlements, tracing the history of development of community and emphasizing the disorganizing effects of changes that bring small communities into close contact with urban centers. These themes—descriptive detail, historical perspective, and emphasis on local effects of contact with the expanding urban world—characterized hundreds of rural community studies over the following decades (see Saunders et al., 1978:55; Smith, 1970). Rural community studies, along with case studies of urban neighborhoods, which also began around 1900, have provided much of the foundation for development of theory in American sociology.

Research in rural sociology began with Charles Josiah Galpin's study of town and country relationships in Walworth County, Wisconsin (1915). His initial research, conducted with surveys and other field methods during the years 1911–1913, asked a series of questions, including: "Is there such a thing as a rural community? If so, what are its characteristics? Can the farm population as a class be considered a community? Or can you cut out of the open country any piece, large or small, square, triangular, or irregular in shape, and plan institutions for them?" (Galpin, 1918:70).

Thus, from the beginning, community research in rural sociology had a practical, applied emphasis. The findings, presented in a series of maps of the service zones of functions provided by village centers to farm families and others in outlying areas, leave little doubt as to the answers. Town and country are not separate rural communities. Together, says Galpin (see Kolb and Brunner, 1952:211), the village and farm residents form a "rurban" community. Moreover, detailed analysis of the different service zones—trade, banking, newspapers, milk industries, churches, schools, libraries, and governments—show the communities of the country to be composite ones with each of them "possessing the characteristic, pulsating instability of all real life" (Galpin, 1918:87).

Galpin's bulletin, *The Social Anatomy of an Agricultural Community* (1915), stimulated a large number of descriptive studies in the 1920s and 1930s by social scientists in land-grant colleges and agricultural experiment stations. Studies by John Kolb (1923, 1925) in Wisconsin, for example, continued the investigation of service relationships between farm and village residents in Walworth County and other counties in the state. Edmund Brunner and associates (Brunner, 1927; Brunner, Hughes, and Patten, 1927; Brunner and Lorge, 1937) undertook a study of 140 agricultural villages in various parts of the country, plotting boundaries of rural–urban interaction networks with methods similar to those employed by Galpin. Similar studies during the same era were conducted in England, Australia, Asia, and Latin America (see Kolb and Brunner, 1952:219-23). Other empirical studies, following Galpin's lead, investigated various aspects of social organization, including social participation, stratification, and community action (see Loomis and Beegle, 1957), and the results of numerous studies were used by Pitirim Sorokin, Carle Zimmerman, and Galpin (1930) to illustrate theoretical arguments about structure and change in rural communities.

The early emphasis on determining the geographic boundaries of rural–urban communities was broadened in the 1930s to consider the effects of the interplay of cultural and ecological factors in community formation and change. One of the most influential studies of this interplay in rural sociology was Lowry Nelson's analysis of the Mormon village, which appeared first as a doctoral dissertation at the University of Wisconsin (Nelson, 1930:11) and later was expanded into a book (Nelson, 1952). His study shows how a religious vision—the Mormon plan for village communities—based on ideology of "communism, millenialism and nationalism" (1930:29) interacted with the physical environment of the Great Basin area of the American West to produce a village form characterized by extraordinary group solidarity. Later research by Evon Vogt and Thomas O'Dea (1953), comparing a Mormon community with a community of non-Mormon settlers in the same area, shows a sharp contrast in collective action styles associated with the difference in values between the two local populations.

The period of greatest activity in community research in rural sociology occurred in the late 1930s and early 1940s in a series of empirical studies sponsored by the Bureau of Agricultural Economics (BEA) of the United States Department of Agriculture. Galpin's work in Wisconsin and subsequent publications by Kolb, Brunner, and others in land-grant universities had paved the way for acceptance of the idea of field work in sociology as a means of compiling useful information on social conditions and trends. In the aftermath of the Great Depression, the BEA, under the leadership of Carl C. Taylor, organized a national project to describe and compare small communities in various regions of the country, with similar methods of data collection and analysis to be used in all of the cases. The best known products of this effort are reports of the "Rural Life Studies," which appeared beginning in 1941. Each report presents "The Culture of a Contemporary Rural Community." The six case studies in this series cover El Cerrito, New Mexico; Sublette, Kansas; Irwin, Iowa; Lancaster, Pennsylvania; Landaff, New Hampshire; and Harmony, Georgia. Each study, using survey data and information collected from a variety of other sources, describes the local ecology, local social organization, and patterns of local social participation. These and other community studies conducted by the BEA (e.g., Lewis, 1948) and by cooperating researchers in land-grant universities provide considerable evidence of differences among rural American communities (Goudy and Ryan, 1982:257), although as pointed out by critics (e.g., Olson, 1964), the contribution of the series would have been greater had there been an explicitly comparative approach in the design of the analyses.

A number of other influential studies by rural sociologists and researchers in related fields appeared in the 1940s and in the 1950s, although by then less emphasis was being placed on comprehensive description of local life than on detailed analysis of specific issues such as stratification (Kaufman, 1944) and action to improve specific services (Miller, 1953).

As the literature of rural sociology grew with descriptive reports from field studies, it also grew with articles and books that were written, as one author puts it, "for those who seek community improvement" (Hoiberg, 1955:ix). Many of the early writers on the rural community in sociology expressed no reservations about the normative and ameliorative objectives of their scientific studies of local social life (see Falk and Gilbert, 1985:563-65), although some (e.g., Sanderson and Polson, 1939) distinguished community organization as an applied activity from the detached and scientific study of community social organization, and others (e.g., Sorokin and Zimmerman, 1929) encouraged the discipline to emphasize the latter over the former. In addition to descriptive case studies, such as Jean and Jess Ogden's (1946) *Small Communities in Action*, rural sociologists and others provided "guideposts for community workers and group leaders" (Sanders, 1950). Many observers in the post-World War II era, of course, wrote of the importance of the search for community in an "age of crisis" (Brownell, 1950; Morgan, 1957; Nisbet, 1953; Stein, 1960).

Even though rural sociology has developed in large part through community studies, the most influential and the best known studies of small towns and small cities have been conducted by researchers outside the field of rural sociology. The "Middletown" studies by Robert and Helen Lynd (1929, 1937) and the "Yankee City" series by Lloyd Warner and associates (e.g., Warner and Lunt, 1941), describing social relationships and changes in stratification and power in small centers, are among these, as are John Dollard's *Caste and Class in a Southern Town*

(1937) and Allison Davis, Burleigh Gardner, and Mary Gardner's *Deep South* (1944). The best known of all of the American community studies, Arthur Vidich and Joseph Bensman's analysis of life in "Springdale" (1958), which describes the effects of the coming of mass society in an agricultural village, cannot be claimed by rural sociology, nor can the studies of "Plainville," a small town in the Ozarks, by James West (1945) and Art Gallaher (1961). Walter Goldschmidt's study of the community effects of agricultural organization (1947), W. F. Cottrell's "Death by Dieselization" (1951), Evon Vogt and Thomas O'Dea's studies of "Homestead" and "Rimrock" (1953), and many other important studies of rural communities have influenced rural sociology and the sociology of the community in general but were not conducted within the field of rural sociology itself. These studies, of course, along with those in rural sociology proper, must be considered in the search for insights into the relationship between community and rural life.

The era of the study of the small community as a microcosm of society was over by the early 1960s. Commenting on this, Irwin Sanders and Gordon Lewis say that "the holistic, thought-provoking studies of an earlier day, studies that provided both good ethnography and a systematic look at communities as complex but meaningful wholes (irrespective of theoretical orientation), seem to have lost their popularity if not their utility" (1976:45). And they add:"It would be comforting, perhaps, if one could say with confidence, 'That cow is dry,' as we turned aside from the task. What one suspects we are hearing is the more defeatist response, 'I've lost interest in milking' " (1976:45). Their review of rural community studies published during 1965–1975, which they compare to the review of studies during 1950–1961 by Thomas Ford and Willis Sutton (1964), poses an important critical question about the future of community research, specifically a question of what would be gained and lost in sociological insights over the years ahead as a result of "scatteration of topics and themes" and the growing popularity of the "formal quantitative approach" (1976:50). The themes they note—delineation of community boundaries; perceptions of community problems; satisfaction with the community; community power and leadership; voluntary organizations and social participation; communications; racial and ethnic structures; local industrial development; responses to environmental issues; and population growth and social change—represent obviously important community phenomena, although studies of these topics tend to concentrate on limited aspects of the whole community. Community-related articles, book reviews, and bulletin listings in the journal *Rural Sociology* over recent years show that the trends in the field noted by Sanders and Lewis have persisted. Research in rural sociology continues to investigate important questions about the community, and much of the research, though narrow in scope, uses sophisticated theories and methods. The fifty-year index to *Rural Sociology* (Garkovich, 1985) lists more than three hundred articles under the headings "community," "community development," "community institutions," and "community processes," and at least fifty of those published since 1975 are empirical studies of some aspect of the rural community. A dozen or so research articles of this type appear in the same period in the *Journal of the Community Development Society*, and perhaps twice that number appear in other scholarly journals. Meanwhile, agricultural experiment stations and extension bulletins and other publications by academic institutions and government research agencies present descriptive information on a large number of community topics. One might say with confidence that the sociology of the community is thriving in rural sociology (Luloff and Swanson, 1990), although comprehensive studies of particular rural communities are virtually unheard of these days (an exception is Ploch, 1989). What the major studies in rural sociology provide is an intensive examination of given aspects of the community, but these are aspects *of* the community and not merely aspects of social life *in* the community.

In this regard, trends in rural sociology stand in contrast to developments in the sociology of the community in general, which is dominated by research in large cities. Following Floyd

Hunter's (1953) pioneering work with the reputational method, the sociology of community turned its attention in the 1950s and 1960s mainly to the identification of community influentials and to measuring the effects of community power structure on policy outputs of governmental and other agencies (see Aiken and Mott, 1970; Clark, 1968; Lyon and Bonjean, 1981). Qualitative case studies were replaced by statistical analyses of data on large samples of cities and metropolitan counties as the study of community power grew to the peak of its popularity around 1970. As attention turned more and more to abstract measurement levels and away from substantive issues in community action and decision-making, this special area of community research lost its appeal and virtually disappeared (see Walton, 1976). Meanwhile, stimulated by J. A. Barnes' (1954) classic qualitative study of interpersonal contacts in a Norwegian fishing village, sociological research in urban neighborhoods began to plot acquaintance networks, and this line of research led to the development and use of space-free concepts of the community, as discussed in the previous chapter. These and other trends represent something other than the "scatteration" of themes one finds in rural studies; they represent to no small degree the demise of the sociology *of* the community in urban studies.

In a sense, this development in urban community research simply reflects the empirical reality of the modern city. The large modern metropolis is a complete local society, but taken as a whole it can hardly be called a community. It is, as Roland Warren (1978:Chapter 13) observes, an arena or stage where highly differentiated interest groups encounter one another in turbulent interactions. Rather than searching for threads of cohesion among the interactions at the center of this stage (i.e., for the connections that would comprise the community field of the city as a whole), urban studies tend to concentrate on other topics and to use the city only as the setting for the study. Smaller local societies, by virtue of their scale, present a somewhat more favorable setting for expecting the community field to emerge as a characteristic of the local society as a whole. Thus, the search for the community, or at least the search for some aspects of the community, is less likely to be undertaken in urban sociology, which studies large cities, than in rural sociology, which studies small towns and rural areas.

Articles in a special issue of *Rural Sociology* in 1978 on "Aspects of the Rural Community" are illustrative of recent themes and research styles in the field of rural community studies. One set of articles, drawn from background research for a proposed project in community education, presents qualitative descriptions and interpretations of selected events and patterns in four small communities—efforts to secure outside resources to meet community needs (Burns, 1978), a taxpayer's revolt precipitated by extensive immigration (Hennigh, 1978), strategies used by local leaders to build ties to the larger society (Clinton, 1978), and episodes of conflict between residents and employees of public agencies (Colfer and Colfer, 1978). Accompanying these, a set of "Other Community Articles" presents a variety of sociological analyses of community-related topics—a study of boundary maintenance in response to tourism development in an Amish community (Buck, 1978), a theoretical analysis of community satisfaction as a dimension of definition of the situation (Deseran, 1978), a statistical analysis of the effects of manufacturing growth on incomes and income distribution in a sample of small urban centers (Rogers et al., 1978), a "contextual" analysis of the effects of community differences on interactions among mine workers (Nelson and Grams, 1978), and an analysis of interactions between local residents and government officials at the district level in Thailand (Haas, 1978). Each of these could be classified under topics other than "community research," and each deals with the community in only one of its many dimensions. Still, each of these addresses an important question about the community itself.

The topics of recent studies in rural communities are similar to those noted in previous reviews. A number of studies measure perceptions and evaluations of community attributes by local residents (e.g., Bachtel and Molnar, 1980; Christenson and

Taylor, 1982; Goudy, 1977, 1983; Maurer and Napier, 1981; Sofranko and Fliegel, 1984; Warner and Burdge, 1979). Community power continues to be a prominent theme (e.g., Beaulieu and Ryan, 1984; Bokemeier and Tait, 1980; Nix et al., 1977; Preston and Guseman, 1979; Williams, 1980). Recent research also addresses questions about organization and participation in community affairs (e.g., Cantrell et al., 1982; Houghland and Sutton, 1978; Houghland et al., 1979; Nowak et al., 1982; Poole, 1981; Rank and Voss, 1982). Community action and development, another persisting theme, receives much attention in recent literature. Qualitative descriptions of actions in small communities (e.g., Moxley, 1985; Ploch, 1976; Preston, 1983), statistical analyses of local actions and government programs in samples of municipalities (e.g., Ham, 1976; Hirschl and Summers, 1982; Israel, 1985; Lloyd and Wilkinson, 1985; Luloff and Wilkinson, 1979; Martin and Wilkinson, 1984; Snipp and Summers, 1981; Wilkinson et al., 1984), and studies of the effects of action programs on community well-being (e.g., Johansen and Fuguitt, 1984:161-82; Krannich and Humphrey, 1983; McGranahan, 1984; Miller et al., 1984; Rogers et al., 1978; Voth et al., 1982) are among the recent contributions. Rural growth in the 1970s (see Fuguitt, 1985) stimulated much research on the growth process itself in small communities (e.g., Christenson and Crouch, 1982; Johansen and Fuguitt, 1984; Luloff and Chittenden, 1984) and on perceived and actual consequences of growth (e.g., Albrecht and Geertsen, 1982; England and Albrecht, 1984; Krannich et al., 1985; Osborne et al., 1984; Price and Clay, 1980). In recent years, as in the past, community studies in rural sociology have often pursued both scholarly and applied objectives, although questions about what constitutes good scholarship and how sociological research can best contribute to rural well-being are open to discussion in the literature (e.g., Gilbert, 1982; Goudy and Ryan, 1982; Summers, 1986; Wilkinson, 1986b).

Moreover, given the rather large number of studies in rural sociology on community-related topics, it is striking that few studies, especially few recent ones, deal explicitly with the rural–community relationship. Some use a measure of rural as one of the independent or explanatory variables, but more often the rural or small town environment serves only as the setting for the study. Consequently, despite the considerable body of literature on various aspects of the community in small towns and rural areas, many questions remain to be answered about precisely how the rural–urban character of the area affects the community.

CRITICAL ISSUES

Reviewers over the years have found much to criticize in the sociological literature on rural communities. Three criticisms in particular point to questions of central importance to this study. These questions concern the scientific quality of research on small communities, the ideological basis of this area of work, and the assumptions commonly made about the effects of rural and urban characteristics on the community and social well-being.

The question of scientific quality appears time and again in reviews of community research in rural and urban settings. August Hollingshead (1948), surveying community research through the late 1940s (much of which was conducted in small towns and rural areas), describes what he calls "the low level of scientific development of the field." He cites deficiencies in clarity of terms, precision of concepts, and theoretical and empirical grounding of propositions. Albert Reiss (1959), a decade later, criticizes the field for failing to distinguish the community from other social phenomena in local settlements. Thomas Ford and Willis Sutton (1964), reviewing studies of rural communities published during the years 1950–1961, find essentially the same flaws reported by Hollingshead and Reiss. They say:

It would be gratifying to be able to conclude from our review of recent community studies that the earlier deficiencies of the field cited by Hollingshead . . . have been largely corrected. Unfortunately, candor forces the concession that his

harsh summary evaluation of the scientific quality of the field
in the late 1940s is still valid today (1964:220).

In particular, they comment on lack of agreement as to the
"generic meaning of community," lack of specification of the
range of major community types, and lack of integration of the
field of community studies in either its theoretical, methodological, or applied dimensions. Phillip Olson (1964), reviewing rural
American community studies sponsored by government agencies
(principally by the United States Department of Agriculture)
through the 1950s, comments on the lack of a theoretical framework, the tendency to concentrate descriptively and superficially
on details, and the absence of any attempt to examine underlying
structural realities. Sanders and Lewis (1976), writing a decade
later, report finding a number of theoretical and methodological
improvements, but they add: "Mindless empiricism—often
poorly done, at that—seems to be a hardy perennial in this field
and is to a degree unjustifiable even by those who might defend
Experiment Station publications done with public funds as providing general information of use to certain lay publics"
(1976:48).

No doubt, a detailed review of studies since the mid-1970s
would show, as some observers suggest (Summers, 1986; Wilkinson, 1986b), that further improvements have been made in
theory, measurement and analysis, although instances of "mindless empiricism" still could be found. Indeed, on many of the
criteria used by earlier reviewers, recent research on community-
related topics shows a fairly high level of scientific development.

Among the remaining deficiencies, however, one is most
important. The field as a whole, despite the use of sophisticated
theory and methods, is no closer in the 1980s than it was in the
1950s to a consensus on the meaning of "rural" and "community." George Hillery (1955:113-15), searching for common
elements among definitions of the community through the mid-
1950s, provides parallel analyses for the "generic community"
and the "rural community," and both analyses reveal a great

variety of meanings in common use. In the 1980s, the meaning of "rural" is still confused, the meaning of "community" is still confused, and when these confusing terms are joined, the problems of definition are compounded. The task of conceptual clarification of the relationship between rurality and community has received little systematic attention as both "rural" and "community" have come to be viewed more as settings for study than as objects of study in sociology. Conceptual confusion, therefore, is a major problem to be faced in using previous literature to help understand the relationship that is of central interest to this study.

Ideology—the body of ideas about the needs and aspirations of people—also has been an issue in rural community research over virtually the entire history of American sociology. The earliest rural community studies were part of the ameliorative-normative movement that gave the discipline of sociology its first foothold in North America (Hollingshead, 1948). The founding of rural sociology clearly was an effort to use science to improve rural community life. Early critics challenged this applied mission, arguing that it could retard scientific development of the discipline (see Falk and Gilbert, 1985:563). Later, as rural sociology came to be institutionalized in land-grant colleges of agriculture, critics questioned the ideology of the field as well as its scientific quality (Anderson, 1959; Olson, 1964). Recent commentaries also call for careful appraisal of the ideological underpinnings of rural community research (e.g., Gilbert, 1982).

Basically the issues have not changed much over the years, although historical and structural conditions have influenced research in rural sociology in obvious ways. According to William Falk and Jess Gilbert (1985), the early rural sociologists had a radical agenda: they wanted to transform rural communities, not simply to understand them, and certainly not to preserve them. According to Olson (1964), government support and bureaucratic standardization led to repression of this agenda, and community research in particular became part of an effort to preserve the existing order by studying it intensely without questioning its

premises and inequalities. Falk and Gilbert (1985:565), seeking
to counter this trend, call for "bringing rural sociology back
in—*from* practical irrelevance, *to* policy issues and debates."
Their call to restore the ameliorative orientation of an earlier
period in rural sociology carries with it, of course, the challenge
to articulate clearly a concept of social well-being—an ideology,
as it were—to give direction to research and praxis.

The third question raised by criticisms of the field concerns
assumptions about the effects of rural and urban variables on the
community and social well-being—assumptions that are of central
interest to this study. Unfortunately, as noted above, the previous
literature reports little research on these effects, although assumptions about the consequences of rural–urban variation and rural-to-
urban change command much attention in the literature. Reviewers,
commenting on both rural sociology and urban sociology, make the
point that untested assumptions about rural–urban variation and about
the process of urbanization in rural areas continue to provoke
confusion in theories of community and social change (e.g., Bender,
1978; Dewey, 1960; Fischer, 1977; Greer, 1962; Gusfield, 1975;
Pahl, 1966; Richards, 1978; Saunders et al., 1978; Wilkinson et al.,
1982). The principal confusion, says Peter Mann (1965:2-4), is in
relating rural–urban to past–present. Partly because of popular essays
on the city by Georg Simmel (1950) and Louis Wirth (1938), a
tendency persists to use contrasting images of modern urban life and
past rural life to explain contemporary differences among communities and to formulate models of the effects of urbanization in rural
areas. Criticisms of this tendency in the literature show clearly that
the field needs a conception of the sociological meaning of rural and
urban variables to apply to modern times. A systematic program of
research also is needed to measure the effects of these variables on
precisely delineated indicators of community and social well-being.

RURAL AND SOCIAL INTERACTION

Controversies in previous literature call for a fresh approach
to assessing the interactional consequences of rural and urban

characteristics of localities. The approach of this study begins with a search for the essential meaning of the phenomenon of "rural." By distinguishing the interactional effects of inherently rural properties from the effects of the other properties of rural areas, an analysis can begin to sort out the various sources of community problems and the potentials for community development in what is called rural America.

The term "rural America," used loosely for convenience (and, to some extent, for effect), is, of course, vague and potentially deceptive. It can direct attention to parts of localities defined as rural by the census bureau (or by some other agency) or to nonmetropolitan counties (which contain both rural and urban areas as defined for the census of population). Usually it refers to some combination of these, such as nonmetropolitan counties *plus* the portions of metropolitan counties outside the central cities and their urbanized fringes. Similarly, we speak of the "rural community" and of "rural community development"; but with the strictures laid down in the previous chapter, there must be some doubt that a community could in fact be rural. A frequent usage is "the community in rural areas," but such a usage begs the question of what makes an area rural and demands an analysis of the connection between rural location and community. The "predominantly rural community," which also is used frequently, has the advantage of recognizing rural as a variable and not a type, although the adjective "predominantly" is not very precise.

What is the essential meaning of "rural?" The number of residents in a local settlement is one guide: the population "not urban" in the census of population is rural; "urban," in turn, means either that there are 2,500 or more residents in a designated place or that the place is within the "urbanized" portion of a metropolitan area. This is a convenient guide, but it hardly suffices to define rural in a sociological sense. What is the fundamental and persisting quality that makes something more or less rural even as its other properties change? Everyday language suggests an answer, but an ambiguous one. Rural comes from *rūs*, the Latin word for room or open space, as does rustic, which means "typical of the country." Rustic, however, also means "simple and unrefined." So long as a simple and unrefined society was typical of the country there was no ambiguity. Unfortunately, in contemporary usage the language asserts, contrary to observation, that what once was typical of life in the country is somehow inherent to rural life. Sociologists have drawn three elements of meaning from these origins (see Willits and Bealer, 1967; Willits, Bealer, and Crider, 1982). An ecological element—few people distributed in a large territory—expresses the original emphasis on space. Ecologically, "rural" once predicted a particular occupational pattern, namely farming (or work in other industries producing raw materials), as the basis of sustenance organization. Historically as well, people in sparsely settled areas often have displayed a distinctive sociocultural pattern, one characterized by adherence to traditional norms and conservative values. Thus, rurality often is taken to mean rural space, farming (or the like) and a traditional lifestyle. Given that these meanings no longer overlap to the degree they once did, a question arises as to which should be taken as the essential meaning of rural? Obviously they all deserve study; but if the three elements are not highly correlated, only one of them should continue to be known as rural.

Observation and common sense give precedence to the ecological meaning of rural (see Dewey, 1960). The other meanings have as their only claim to this label the assumption that they once were typical of life in many ecologically rural areas. None of the traditionally rural industries, as these are practiced in modern societies, can be said to be rustic in the sense of being simple or unrefined. To the contrary, farming, forestry, and other extractive industries tend to use sophisticated technologies and a complex form of social organization. It is true, of course, that much of the work in these takes place in ecologically rural areas, but it is not true that they provide the principal means of support of the residents of rural areas. And while farmers, among others, might still tend to follow traditional and conservative patterns, such patterns are as likely to be found in large population centers as in more rural areas. To call an occupation or a lifestyle rural is misleading in modern America. The original meaning derived from *rūs* must take precedence in designating the ecological meaning as the essential one.

Rural, therefore, is a territorial concept. This is a most important consideration for the study of rural life and the community because the community, as conceptualized in the previous chapter, has a territorial base. The study of rural life and community, therefore, is the study of the associations between one essential element of the community (i.e., the territorial element) and other essential elements of the community.

The territorial concept of rural needs further specification and refinement to be useful in sociology. The land itself is not the point of sociological interest. What is of interest is the arrangement of people and activities on the land. Rural, as a sociological variable, refers to the extent of dispersion of people in a local ecology. Dispersion is of sociological importance because of its presumed effects on the interactions of people.

In contrast to this view, Howard Newby (1980), critically reviewing the field of rural sociology, says bluntly that a territorial conception of the essential nature of rural identifies a variable that has no usefulness in modern sociology. Rural describes nothing but a geographic setting for social life by his account, and rural sociology, therefore, is no more needed to study social life in this spatial context than would be, say, "Tuesday sociology" to study social life in a particular temporal context. At issue, of course, is a question as to the effect of the setting on social behavior.

In this study, the setting is assumed to have important effects. With the conception of the community as a social field, the context (in its spatial and temporal dimensions) can never be separated from the processes of social interaction that define it as a context (see Wilkinson, 1970b). Thus, the context and the action can be said to "affect" one another because actually they create and embody one another. The question to be addressed, therefore, in assessing the sociological importance of the essential, spatial

meaning of rural, is whether the actions in one context (one that
is more or less rural than others) differ systematically from the
actions in other contexts because of the contextual effects.
Whether rural sociology is needed is an empirical question from
this perspective.

THE RURAL–URBAN LOCALITY

The direct effects of rural location on community interaction
and social well-being should be studied in the locality, the area
of local life where people meet their daily needs together. Far
from being merely the geographic setting of social life, the
locality is the spatial manifestation of a fundamental organization
of interdependencies among people. How rural the locality is,
therefore, is a key factor for determining the characteristics and
effectiveness of social organization.

As Amos Hawley (1950:258) maintains, "the daily rhythm of
collective life" gives unity and distinctiveness to a local population as a social organization, notwithstanding the integration of
the population into organizational structures that extend beyond
the locality. This daily rhythm consists of interrelated activities
through which people meet their needs together. From a spatial
standpoint, says Hawley, "The community may be defined as
comprising that area the resident population of which is interrelated and integrated with reference to its daily requirements"
(1950:257).

Organization is a contribution of the locality, and organization
is what rural location affects directly. Considering interdepen-
dence alone, as Hawley notes, the nation or even the world can
be viewed as one large system, at least in some respects; but when
attention turns to the organization of the multiple interdependencies that compose everyday life, analysis must turn to the locality
where people actually live together.

A most important consideration for examining the influence of
rural location on social organization is the recognition that
localities rarely are either exclusively rural or exclusively urban.

Rural and urban are not types but variables. Localities tend to be both rural and urban: they are rural-urban or, as Charles Galpin (1915) suggests, "rurban." In other words, the locality, where people meet their various needs together, typically includes both an outlying area of diffuse settlement and a more compact central area (or areas) where many daily needs are served. The central areas are easy to find because interrelationships among activities encourage concentration of settlement. The outlying area is not so easy to delineate; its borders pose a perennial problem for community research. One still must ask, just as Galpin (1915) did, where people go for work, services, and other regular contacts. Approaching this problem from the perspective of those in outlying areas, Galpin surveyed farm residents to determine their connections with readily visible centers, and then he used the results to plot the distances covered by daily movements to and from centers. His findings and those of countless subsequent studies describe not rural and urban localities but rural-urban localities. With few exceptions (such as a truly isolated and self-sufficient homestead), people who live in what we call rural areas actually live in rural-urban localities.

As a concept, the rural-urban locality is much more useful than such alternative notions as the rural-urban dichotomy and the rural-urban continuum. The rural-urban dichotomy is outmoded and its use as a scientific concept often belies a value bias. The rural-urban continuum is simply an inaccurate description of the diverse and fluid reality of rural-urban localities. It is more appropriate to treat rural and urban as variable characteristics of all localities than as locality types.

Research on the effects of ruralness in rural-urban localities, of course, calls for an operational decision as to the limits of the outlying area and then for calculation of the proportions of rural and urban within the locality as a whole. Delineation of the limits of the whole and subdivision into rural and urban components require careful deliberation and cautious judgments because these operations impose order on an essentially unbounded and constantly changing field of social interactions. Once made, however, these necessary decisions clear the way for analysis of rural as a factor in community life.

RURAL COMMUNITY LIFE

Rural location can influence community interaction, at least nominally, by influencing the probability of interpersonal contacts within the local population. As observed in geography, human ecology, and group dynamics (see Mayhew and Levinger, 1976; Olsson, 1965), distance affects the probability of contact. Specifically, as distance increases, the probability of contact goes down. Contact technologies such as automobiles and telephones can reduce this effect of distance, but never to zero (Mayhew and Levinger, 1976:94). The probability of contact between persons tends to diminish as the distance between them increases.

Applying this to community interaction, rural population dispersion as a locality characteristic can be said to structure opportunities for contact among local residents. The greater the degree of dispersion, the greater the average distance between residents. The greater the distance, the lower the probability of contact. Thus, rural dispersion exerts a drag effect on contacts in the local ecology.

Observation, however, shows that specifying the level of analysis and the type of contact is crucial to the validity of this proposition. At the community level, rural dispersion depresses the probability function for the overall volume of contacts (e.g., between all possible dyads), but at the individual level, this need not affect the probability that one would have contacts with immediate neighbors, friends, or relatives. There is no good reason for expecting the total number of close and intimate contacts per person to differ greatly between more or less urbanized areas (Kasarda and Janowitz, 1974). As dispersion increases, what decreases is not the probable number of close and intimate contacts, but the number of contacts that are distant. This has a most important direct effect on the probability of contacts with strangers: as rural dispersion increases contacts in "weak ties" tend to decrease.

Mark Granovetter's (1973) essay on "The Strength of Weak Ties" gives definitions and suggestions, as mentioned earlier, for studying this effect, although his own analysis deals with urban networks. The strength of an interpersonal tie, he says, is a "combination of the amount of time, the emotional intensity, the intimacy (mutual confiding), and the reciprocal services which characterize the tie" (1973:1361). Strong ties involve repeated contacts and relatively intimate exchanges. A weak tie is transitory and impersonal. He argues that both kinds of relationships contribute to social stability and social well-being. Without weak ties to bind strong ties into the larger structure of the community, the strong ties in parts of the community could restrict opportunities for upward mobility of people and contribute to disruption of the community as a whole.

Using these concepts, one can argue that the effect of rural dispersion is to depress the probability of weak ties and thus to increase the proportion of all contacts among strong ties. Distance, which is an indispensable feature of rural life, is the reason. If Granovetter is correct in his assessment of the contribution of weak ties to community structure and social well-being, a rural settlement pattern can be a source of community problems.

Granovetter's argument in network theory is similar to earlier theories in sociology. As noted previously, Emile Durkheim's thesis about the influence of material density on moral density can be interpreted as having the same implications. Material density would be low under conditions of "mechanical" solidarity, he says, but "organic" solidarity requires a high level of material density. This is because relatively isolated agrarian settlements in the past could sustain local social organization through "mechanical causes and impulsive forces, such as affinity of blood, attachment to the same soil, ancestral worship, and community of habits" (1933:278); but the complex division of labor in modern societies requires extensive interaction among diverse groupings within and among localities. Moral density,

Durkheim's term for such interaction, depends on material density. Where material density is low, as in outlying areas, solidarity is impaired. Although Durkheim's analysis of modern society gives little attention specifically to the question of rural–urban location and community, his thesis implies that rural characteristics would restrict the kind of interactions that are necessary to sustain a modern community field.

This argument also agrees with propositions about adaptive capacity and community stability in human ecology. From the ecological perspective, the organization of the community is a property "that has evolved and is sustained in the process of adaptation of the population to its environment, which may include other populations" (Duncan and Schnore, 1959:136). To be effective, the community's organization must be able to meet the daily needs of residents and adapt to changes in the environment (Hawley, 1971:11). This, according to Hawley's general theory of human ecology (1950), requires two kinds of collective action, namely, the co-action of like forms (commensalism) and the co-action of unlike forms (symbiosis). Where either is deficient, the ability of the community organization to meet local needs and adapt to environmental changes is impaired. Urbanization provides differentiation and integration of unlike forms, and in this way urbanization, at least up to some threshold, contributes to increasing the adaptive capacity of the community (see Hauser, 1965:19).

Thus, population dispersion encourages contacts to be predominantly in primary relationships, not because of a rural cultural preference, but because contacts are missing in other kinds of important relationships. This is a deficit and not a strength of rural social life. Adaptive capacity is impaired by lack of diversity in community structure, and local well-being is depressed as a consequence.

Before discussing specific consequences for the community field, a second potential effect of rural characteristics needs to be mentioned. Ruralness also could increase the potential for contacts to be integrated into a holistic network or field. There are two reasons for this. First, problems of integration increase with the total number of contacts. Fewer contacts mean fewer problems of coordination and a greater probability that the activities in various contacts will influence one another and form a holistic field. People in a rural area, for example, are likely to encounter one another in many different roles, such as parent–teacher, merchant–customer, official–constituent, and so on; and their activities in various contacts are likely to reflect this fact. Second, rural life encourages integration among contacts by increasing the probability that these contacts will be repeated and intimate; that is, that they will be in strong ties, which, nominally at least, have some degree of integration. Although integration among strong ties gives no assurance that the local society as a whole will be an integrated community, some advantages for the formation of community can be found in this implication of rural location. Strong ties encourage community even though the shortage of weak ties might work against community. The scale of social life associated with rural location thus presents both problems and opportunities for community development.

These nominal implications of rural space give no more than a point of departure for the task of unraveling the association between rural–urban location and social interaction. Integration depends upon much more than the opportunity structures for strong and weak ties. For one thing, the two sets of implications mentioned above can be offsetting. Rural location can depress crucial interactions, but it also promises to foster connections among interactions. For another thing, the effects of distance and scale are potential effects and not inevitable consequences of rural dispersion. The drag effect of distance can be mitigated by technology and other developments, and the advantages of small-scale social organization can be suppressed by structural cleavages and by other factors. Moreover, the effects of rural–urban variation can combine with the effects of other variables to influence social interaction.

Considering the many factors that typically accompany rural dispersion in modern society, the one that stands out most dramatically as a factor in community interaction and social well-being is seen in high rates of poverty and inequality in predominantly rural areas (Joint Economic Committee, 1986). One reason is that these areas have been "left behind" (Whiting, 1974) in the historical development of a complex urban-based society. As the national economy became largely industrial and the culture became essentially urban in the history of the United States, many small communities found themselves at a disadvantage for meeting the needs of residents. A small, localized economy could no longer be self-sufficient, and the number of people required to justify sophisticated and expensive service delivery systems increased. Sparsity of settlement and distance from centers of economic growth have become major sources of socioeconomic problems in many rural localities (Warner, 1974).

In addition to the problems of access to resources, some observers attribute spatially-based inequalities to exploitative tendencies in capitalist development (see Gilbert, 1982; Howes and Markusen, 1981; Lovejoy and Krannich, 1982; Walker, 1978). From urban centers, according to this view, capitalists mobilize, extract, and concentrate surplus production from labor and other resources in peripheral areas. The capitalists make decisions to benefit themselves, regulating the flow of resources into and out of particular areas, assigning special uses to given spaces and drawing selectively on reserve resources in the peripheries as they search for profits. These devices—capital mobility, assignment of specialized uses to spaces, and strategic use of reserves—contribute, according to many critics of modern development (see Wilkinson, 1989), to dependency, instability and underdevelopment in rural areas.

Carl Kraenzel (1955, 1980) suggests the term "social cost of space" to cover both the effects of isolation and the effects of outside manipulation of resources. This combination, he says, produces an unstable economic base and a dearth of local services and facilities in small remote localities. These problems contribute to intergroup hostilities and other barriers to local cooperation. The result is an inability to conduct cooperative community projects. His idea that space has a "social cost" counters the romantic view of rural community life expressed in some previous literature.

Consequences for development and maintenance of a community field follow from these general observations about the effects and correlates of rural–urban variation. In a nutshell, rural is a barrier to emergence of community. Community, as argued earlier, requires a locality where people can meet their daily needs together and a local society where social contacts can produce a holistic structure. As rural dispersion increases, prospects recede for meeting these requirements. Rural life works against the community field by restricting the probability that a complete local society will develop and persist in the immediate area of residence of people in outlying districts. Instead, the larger territory over which people travel to meet their needs becomes in fact their locality; then within the rural–urban locality, rural dispersion impedes the emergence of the community field in two ways. First, distance, restricts the kinds of contacts needed to build community bonds among residents of the local society as a whole. Second, poverty and inequality, which tend to vary positively with rural dispersion, can produce cleavages that block and distort community interaction. Notwithstanding the potential benefits of rural living, barriers to community interaction and social well-being tend to increase in strength as the extent of rural dispersion of the local population increases.

From the standpoint of the more rural segment of the local population, these barriers are at a minimum level when the locality covers a relatively small territory and includes a center (or centers) of sufficient scale to support a wide range of associations for meeting work, service, and related needs. Conditions are less favorable for community interaction as the size of territory increases, which it must do in many cases to support a complete local society. With the decline of small and medium-sized centers in some parts of the United States, the size of territory required for a local society has increased beyond the point where the community as a holistic field of local social interaction is likely to persist, much less to flourish in effective community actions. While the exact numbers are not available, aggregate trends in demographic and economic characteristics of the nonmetropolitan population indicate that residents of many, and perhaps most, predominantly rural localities face what can only be called a crisis of community (Wilkinson, 1988).

Given these conditions and trends, a pressing question for rural sociology is that raised at the beginning of this discussion: Why continue to focus on the rural community and rural community development? Why study and promote an interactional phenomenon that extant trends oppose and might even rule out for large areas of the countryside? The following chapter gives part of the answer by elaborating the concept of social well-being and relating it to the concepts of community and rural. This sets the stage and suggests an agenda for studying and encouraging the process of community development in rural localities.

3

The Community and Rural Well-Being

As an interaction process in the local society, the community contributes directly and positively to the social well-being of local residents. Chapter 2 argues that rural characteristics of the locality suppress community interaction, and this reduces social well-being. This chapter elaborates these propositions by focusing on the concept of social well-being, the relationship between social well-being and community, and the effects of rural location on well-being via its effects on community interaction. The result is a conceptualization of fundamental problems of rural life in modern society that need to be addressed in sociological research and in community development. A realistic appraisal of rural life and social well-being must be the first item on an agenda for either research or action to address the problems of community life in the American countryside.

SOCIAL WELL-BEING

The concept of social well-being as used here depends upon but differs from concepts of individual and ecological well-being (see Wilkinson, 1973). Social well-being individual well-being, and ecological well-being are concepts at different levels of analysis of the same events and processes in empirical reality. Thus, these concepts need to be defined in ways that are consistent with one another. Otherwise the definition at any level will be inadequate. Of particular importance, the unity of the reality base to which the concepts refer at different levels makes it inappropriate to define either one of these as a state of well-being that degrades or constrains well-being at the other levels. Social well-being, individual well-being, and ecological well-being complement and depend upon one another, in the abstract at least. This means well-being of the individual is required for social well-being and is therefore a criterion with which to assess the prospects for social well-being in a given community setting, be it rural or urban. Individual well-being is affected proximally and crucially, of course, by private experiences in intimate relations; and for the most part these experiences are outside the scope of such strategies for improving social well-being as local economic development, service development, and other common forms of social planning. Probably the most effective action at the social level would be to create and maintain "humane" institutional and organizational structures within which the individual's own capacity for well-being in private relations can be liberated (see Goodman, 1956; Schumacher, 1973). The social level can contribute best to individual well-being by freeing the individual from constraints to self-actualization (see Maslow, 1954). In the humanistic psychologies of Gordon Allport (1955) and Abraham Maslow (1954) individual well-being is a natural state that emerges when the person is freed sufficiently from the demands of reducing chemical deficits—what Allport calls the "lower-order needs"—to allow pursuit of distinctively human purposes, particularly the purposes referred to as "higher-order needs," such as social responsiveness and solidarity and the motive of self-actualization. In some circumstances, the dominant constraints to individual well-being are unmet needs for primary resources such as food and safety. In other circumstances, social and ecological conditions provide for these needs adequately, thus allowing human attention and energy to address social issues. Identification of the distinctively social motives and needs to which attention turns beyond the threshold of adequacy of the arrangements for meeting other needs is, of course, of central importance to understanding the role of community interaction in social well-being.

The most distinctively human qualities of the individual are social, interactional qualities. As George Mead's theory of "mind, self, and society" points out, the individual as a person and the structure of the individual's subjective experience of self are themselves aspects or phases of processes of social interaction. The self is an image of interaction and of roles and behaviors in interaction. This is an interpersonal structure, and its meaning connects the nonsocial aspects of the individual's being to the ongoing processes we call society. This interpersonal structure is not reducible to biotic or physiological qualities of the individual or even to psychological processes and structures: the self arises, has meaning, persists, and changes in social interaction.

This interpersonal structure that the social individual experiences as self obviously is influenced by the conditions for meeting lower-order needs and by the social aspects of the processes of social interaction. Self might be experienced partially or in distorted form if, for example, local conditions were such as to cause lower-order needs to occupy one's full energies and divert attention away from self-reflection. Respect, as this term is used in interactional theories (for example, by James, 1910), refers to the accuracy of perception of the social relationships that comprise the self. Respect for one's self and respect for others go together, and respect for human life is but a general case of the same thing. Self-respect can be lacking because of the demands of the lower-order needs, and disrespect can result from inaccurate perceptions. As Erich Fromm (1947, 1956) points out, alienation from the interpersonal basis of one's real self produces ontological insecurity and interpersonal hostility, and these pervert and block natural human qualities of interpersonal warmth, cohesiveness, and respect.

Social conditions, therefore, play an important role, if not an all-powerful role, in individual well-being. The most important social conditions for this purpose are those that minimize interferences with natural processes of individual and interindividual consciousness. It is important to remember, however, that social conditions only set the stage. Avoiding undue emphasis on the social factors as driving forces in well-being can be achieved by emphasizing their negative contributions: certain social conditions can interfere with the natural processes that constitute individual well-being. Without this interference, well-being occurs naturally.

Basically, these negative contributions can be minimized if social arrangements meet two requirements. First, provisions must be adequate to meet sustenance needs. That is, a threshold must be achieved in meeting needs for food, safety, and so on—the lower-order needs—through social relationships. Otherwise people will not be free from the primary struggle for survival. Second, the social processes and structures through which these needs are met and through which other collective interests are pursued must produce minimum interference with accurate personal and interpersonal perception and responses.

The sustenance needs demand first attention, and the first of these is to supply sufficient caloric and other resources to ensure survival of physiological systems and optimal homeostatic functioning of people in their environment. At the social level this demand generalizes to needs for jobs, income, markets, homes, and a range of services. With these needs more or less met to some threshold of adequacy, attention turns to minimizing the proportion of energy that must be given to maintaining need fulfillment at the threshold level or above. Strategies and technologies can be developed to increase efficiency of food production, work organization, service delivery, and the like. These developments have a liberalizing effect to the extent that they free human attention and energy for addressing the higher-order, social needs.

Much of what is called development, particularly much of what is called economic development, especially in rural areas, is concerned almost exclusively with this sustenance category. Development often means economic growth, and the surplus achieved by growth often is to be plowed back into the development process to build infrastructure for more or sustained economic growth. Similarly, rural development strategies that emphasize services and service delivery rarely look beyond the services to ask what comes next. Much attention in applied research in sociology, as in other social science disciplines, has been given to improving service delivery and to anticipating the future service needs of changing communities. These obviously are pressing concerns, and the well-being needs of people are such, especially in small towns and rural areas, to demand that attention be given to them before addressing the more purely social needs. To date, however, development-oriented research for rural America has given far less attention than justified to the question of what comes after the meeting of basic economic and service needs.

What should happen in theory and in policy when the hypothetical sustenance threshold is approached? How much is enough? How much income and what level and quality of services are required? What are the well-being consequences of exceeding the levels actually needed to free human attention and energy from the sustenance quest?

Perhaps effort should continue so as to exceed the threshold and end forever the threat of falling below it. Perhaps, on the other hand, attention should be turned away from the lower-order needs at some point. Critics of the continued emphasis on growth and development in modern industrial and post-industrial societies (see Morrison, 1983; Odum, 1970) warn against the ecological and social consequences of this path. Ecologically, the warning is that unless the growth-oriented path is abandoned in favor of a balance-oriented path, human actions surely will deplete vital natural resources and undermine the basis for virtually any form of social life. The social consequences of the growth-oriented path are equally foreboding (see Schumacher, 1973).

Beyond the point at which basic needs are met to at least an adequate degree, the contribution of continued growth in the capacity to meet these needs diminishes and becomes, at some point, a negative contribution even to the chances of survival. Economic growth can become obsessive hoarding. Proliferation of services and amenities becomes an unnecessary drain on resources, and this fuels divisive competition for symbols of luxury and superiority. In the unrestrained quest for ever higher levels of material acquisition, as Emile Durkheim (1951), observes, one finds both a threat to group survival and a source of extreme alienation from "truly collective experience." Alienation in the quest for affluence alters the natural quality of interpersonal responses. Economic and service development beyond the level of need captures human energy rather than freeing it. Where protection and enhancement of material holdings becomes a dominant social activity, community and the human potential for well-being it supports can be said to fade into the background if not to disappear entirely from social interaction. "Too much" can be as damaging as "too little," even though the criterion points for these judgments can be identified only in abstract terms.

Certainly, then, the meeting of sustenance and related needs, while important to the social conditions for individual well-being, is not a sufficient social condition for this purpose. At the least, there also must be liberation from such additional hindrances as obsession with wealth and growth. Using again the concept of respect to denote a necessary process in individual well-being, these post-sustenance obsessions in a society or culture can be viewed as denying, as it were, the real facts of human social being, especially the fact that economic development and services are means and not ends of individual and social well-being. History, perhaps, is partly to blame, because relative freedom from deficits in access to food and other primary resources and services is still a new experience for a significant portion of Earth's population. A post-sustenance consciousness might be emerging slowly as primary threats to well-being recede for people in some parts of the world, although other threats have emerged to fill the void. A distinctively human era in history might be just over the horizon, but barriers to the emergence of that era are readily apparent in the present.

The transition from a social life oriented mainly toward lower-order needs to a social life oriented mainly toward higher-order needs would contribute to aggregate individual well-being in ways that now are obvious; but what in addition to adequacy of resources for meeting the lower order needs would be the factors needed to facilitate or bring about that shift? What social conditions would be required to give maximum support to individuals in the post-sustenance quest for well-being? Five conditions can be suggested (drawing on Wilkinson, 1973) as the social dimensions or elements of social well-being, and these can be used to elaborate the relationship between the community and social well-being.

Distributive justice. Equity-in-exchange as a concept of social welfare appears in the abstract in virtually all normative systems (see Gouldner, 1960) and in most critical and evaluative frameworks in sociology and related fields (see Habermas, 1970, 1971). Almost all economic development schemes endorse equality and justice, in rhetoric if not in practice (Heady, 1972). Equity in a broader sense than equity-in-exchange refers to human recognition and endorsement of the ultimate *fact* of human equality, a fact underlying even the most uneven systems of distribution of access to such goods as material resources, life chances, and prestige. People are equally human, and recognition of this simple fact, along with the incorporation of this recognition into purposive actions to remove inequalities, would facilitate communication and encourage affirmative, accurate interpersonal responses.

Open communication. Openness refers both to the efficiency of channels for transmitting information and resources among people and to the extent of honesty, completeness, and authenticity of the exchanges in communicative relationships. Communication obviously is the fundamental element of human social interaction. It is an instrument for achieving tasks and also for creating and maintaining the relationships among people that operate to produce social well-being. Open communication is essential to self-respect and respect for others. Anything impeding the flow of communication among people whose lives are connected in other ways impedes social well-being. Full and authentic communication underlies the development of well-being of the individual and of the community.

Tolerance. Acceptance of differences as well as similarities among humans is a shared value among people and one with a decided effect on the interactions among them. Acceptance means respect. Tolerance of others by the individual is, therefore, a component of individual well-being, and tolerance as a shared normative standard of behavior is a social condition that supports well-being.

Collective action. Social well-being entails people working together in pursuit of their common interests. This is a factor in achieving particular goals and in solving particular problems, but it also is a process of building social relationships. At the local level it is the foundation of the community. The community, as a field of social interactions oriented to local issues and concerns, exists in, and thus is a factor in, the collective actions of local residents. It can exist in community conflicts as well as in cooperative episodes. Collective actions expressing the entire range of common locality-oriented interests can be interconnected by actors, associations, and activities in the community field; and to the extent this occurs it promotes and enriches the collective life of a population.

Communion. Accepting Herman Schmalenbach's (1961) distinction between community and celebration of community, the latter can be designated, along with collective action and other forms of actual interaction, as a factor in social well-being. Consciousness of community and joyful response to the relationships that are realized, where these exist in fact rather than simply as ideology, sham, or demand, can contribute to social well-being by encouraging equity, openness, tolerance, and collective action. Communion in the true sense represents an opening of consciousness and of the emotional life of a people to the relationships that already exist among them. With communion, self arises and common, shared purpose becomes a factor in subsequent social interaction. Purposive involvement means escape from bondage and avoidance of alienation through willful selection and creation of community (see Fromm, 1956). Actual, willful entry into and celebration of social relationships are the hallmarks of Maslow's (1954) concept of self-actualization. Communion signifies these acts, as does community development.

Social and individual well-being cannot be achieved, however, according to the argument of this study, except in ways that also promote ecological well-being. Ecological well-being, which in a literal sense means the well-being of the "house" of civilization, refers explicitly to natural and other conditions that support and sustain human life. It is not accurate or appropriate to treat the environment as though it were somehow separate from the social life it supports. An active interdependency characterizes the relationship between social life and its surroundings. Open-systems theories in many disciplines including sociology emphasize these interconnections and show the fragility of conventional concepts of system boundaries. References to human/environment separation cannot be justified on any grounds today, if they might have been justified heuristically in the distant past.

There is, of course, no absolute or inherent basis on which ecological well-being can be judged. Judgments instead rest on assumptions about ecological conditions for social and individual well-being. Taking this humanist approach, a question can be entertained as to whether there are natural ecological limits to what can be attained in social and individual well-being. The value stance of the humanist and the premises of the concept of well-being in this study support the assertion that there are no such limits, but assurance that this is the case is hard to find in the trends of the times. These trends include degradation of air and water quality, the dwindling of plant and animal varieties in nature, the assaults on wilderness and wetland areas, and numerous other signs of a struggle between human civilization and the ecology it inhabits. From the well-being perspective in this study, the key to correcting these assaults on the foundation of the house in which we must live is to hasten the shift from social patterns that serve the lower-order needs to those that serve the higher-order needs. In other words, community development is needed to promote social well-being, and community development also will promote the development of responsible attitudes and practices toward the natural environment.

It is one thing to say community as the epitome of social well-being encourages ecological and individual well-being and quite another thing to determine what exactly could be done to head off the apparent demise of social and individual well-being in the face of a deteriorating ecology for human life. Beyond the obviously important efforts to limit unnecessary economic growth and technological proliferation, and beyond efforts to alter or mediate direct assaults on fragile ecosystems, what can be done, for example, to reduce the massive inequalities among groupings of people within and among communities? Historically, distributive justice, open communication, tolerance, collective action capacity, and other components of what we call social well-being have been mainly the concerns of elite groupings, partly because only the elite have experienced substantial freedom from the sustenance quest. In one sense, history has set the stage for a test in the modern era of the hypothesis that social well-being can be maximized for all or most people through community development without destroying the ecological nest in which human well-being must be nurtured. Models of social well-being for the future clearly must consider ecological well-being as a parameter.

THE COMMUNITY AND SOCIAL WELL-BEING

Whether in national policy or in the purposive activities of people in some specific locality, community development is justified by the assumption that it contributes to social well-being. Vague assertions to this effect and ad hoc lists of the presumed contributions appear regularly in the introductory sections of program documents that describe the objectives and procedures of alternative approaches to community development (see Christenson and Robinson, 1989). Few studies, however, spell out the actual effects of community development in theory, and fewer still can cite data to document effects. Consequently, the literature on community development suffers from a surplus of unsupported claims and biases and from a lack of systematic theory and evidence. The framework suggested by the interactional conception of community and the propositions about social well-being in this chapter can be used to organize research on this topic and to guide community development efforts that have improved social well-being as a goal.

The community is an important factor in social well-being for a number of reasons, some of which have been mentioned in describing the interactional theory of community and in specifying social interaction as the arena where social well-being occurs (see Wilkinson, 1979). First, the community is important for social well-being because the community is where the individual and the society meet. Rene Konig (1968) gives a masterful account of this meeting and a detailed analysis of its implications for socialization and social control. He notes the importance of the family as the first line of contact between the child, on the one hand, and the rules, values, and structures of the society, on the other. This, he says, is only the primary contact; and while it obviously is one of great importance, it is a sharply limited form of contact in which one institution—the family—screens and conveys selected information and selected demands from the outside world. In contrast, the community is a "global" society, a complete network of institutions. When the individual moves beyond the family, the whole of society, in microcosm, comes into range. The person can contact representative components of all of the institutions directly in the local society. Moreover, Konig remarks, the community is the only global unit the individual can engage directly as a totality. At national and multinational levels, "society" is an abstraction; at the local level it is experienced in contacts with real people. At the larger, abstract levels, the individual's direct contacts tend to be in component structures, such as specific organizations; at the local level, contacts in many different components cluster together in time and space. The community therefore is the largest and most comprehensive unit of society in the direct experience of the individual. The importance of this is in the immediacy of the range of contacts available to the individual. Considering both qualities— the immediacy and the range of contacts—as indicative of the potential for social interaction to occur, the community can be said to be not only an important setting for social well-being but to be in fact the most important setting. The community represents a broad range of the direct interpersonal contacts that produce social well-being.

A related contribution of the community (as noted above) is that of providing the interactive locus of the emergence of the self. Self, as Mead (1934) argues, is an interactional phenomenon consisting of the identification of the person in specific interactional relationships with others and in relationship with the "generalized other," or community. As the self is a principal vehicle of social well-being, the community is important because it supplies the field of interactions in which self arises and has its meaning and effects.

In addition, the community is an arena for expressing fundamental human dispositions such as the disposition to associate with other people and the disposition to join with others in cooperative actions. Whether association is taken as a need or simply as a fact of being human, it is a truism that the well-being of people generally depends more that anything else on contacts with other human beings. Association is of both instrumental and intrinsic value to social well-being, and the community is a principal arena of interpersonal association. Other arenas also are important, especially in modern society. Still, the community is the arena of association in which most people have most of their contacts, and it is an area in which almost all people have some important associations.

The opportunity to engage in cooperative, collective actions on behalf of the community as a whole can be taken, following

Durkheim's (1951) discussion of the importance of collective involvement, as a parameter of social well-being. The logic for this is in the idea that collective action represents and validates the self as an active contributor to the process of improving a shared life. Working with others on a community project can affirm one's sense of social responsibility and esteem, and it can contribute to improving material conditions of the shared life as well. Recognizing that important questions need to be raised about whether community action can occur in modern societies, there is no question that if they do occur they can enhance the well-being of those involved.

Further, the concept of well-being in this study rests on the premise that social well-being encourages actions that also protect ecological well-being. While this is an untested argument, it expresses a central humanist postulate of ecological theory, namely the postulate that well-being is a quality of the ecosphere as a whole and not a quality that can be raised in any one part of the whole at the expense of the well-being of the other parts. Following this logic, a hypothesis about community development and protection of the natural environment can be stated as follows: community development (i.e., development of community in a population) reduces the probability of occurrence of actions that degrade ecological well-being.

These contributions of community occur in a complex setting today. It seems clear, as many students of the community have noted, that the needs and wishes of people cannot and should not be met fully through local interaction, and it is certain that behaviors and identities of people are oriented to action fields outside the locality. Moreover, if community is a natural disposition, as claimed here, what about conflict, exploitation, and alienation? Are not these natural as well? The case can be made that anti-community processes are as natural as community, although to make such a case would not rule out the community itself as a natural disposition, and it also would not rule out the contributions community can make. Even if forces contrary to community also are natural, the fact remains that community is experienced mainly on site, and self-actualization depends on authentic, direct interaction among people who live together. Thus the community is important to social well-being because it is an important setting for expression of associational tendencies, and it is an effective process for developing individual competencies in collective action. Community action allows the individual to participate purposively in the creation and articulation of social structures. The range of interest fields one can engage in the community field provides contacts and experiences for broadening individual competencies in social interaction. Through community involvement, therefore, opportunities for self-actualization and well-being can be pursued.

Relationships similar to community but lacking in key community characteristics can be expected to make less substantial contributions to well-being. Some of these relationships are of particular importance in small towns and rural settings. For example, strong ties and intimate networks in some isolated villages give the appearance of community but lack the qualities of equity, openness, tolerance, and collective action that make community interaction a vital force in well-being. Where relationships are close out of necessity and where outside contacts are weak, there is a tendency, noted in case studies by Carol Bly (1981) and others, for the interactions to lose authenticity and for myths to destroy perceptions of actual community conditions. A challenge for community development in such a setting is to help create the conditions for liberating people from the bondage of isolation. Action is needed to reduce rural deprivations so people can experience a more vibrant and rewarding field of community relationship in their local interactions. Another example of a community-like relationship that falls short of providing the conditions for social well-being is one dominated by outside interests or by a powerful elite. Another is the setting where stratification and cleavages block and stifle the interactions among population segments whose lives in fact are bound up together in the local society. Still another is the partial community—a setting that lacks one or more of the common social institutions. Community-like relationships might occur in total institutions such as prisons and military camps (see Hillery, 1968), but lacking the comprehensiveness of life in the local society, the actual experience of community in such a setting is sharply restricted. These and other examples point to barriers to community development and barriers to social well-being.

RURAL WELL-BEING

How does rural well-being stack up against the criteria of social well-being discussed above? In particular, if community is a major vehicle for the achievement of social well-being, as argued here, and if rural life impedes the development and maintenance of the community field, as argued in the previous chapter, what then are the consequences of rural life for social well-being? Theory gives only a general answer, but an ominous one that departs radically from popular images of life in small towns and rural areas. Data on rural trends in the United States leave little doubt as to the strength of associations between rural location and indicators of material well-being. Jobs and income, services, and equality of access to these and other resources are associated negatively with the rural character of localities (see Joint Economic Committee, 1986). Deficits in these give direct evidence of problems of social well-being. From the theoretical perspective of this discussion they also forebode critical problems in local social interaction.

Rural sociology has been slow to investigate possible associations between rural residence and problems in the quality of social relationships. Much more attention has been given to problems of rural poverty and service delivery and to studies of stratification and rural inequality than to personal and social disruptions associated with rural life. One reason perhaps is well-founded scientific caution about attributing some extreme forms of disruption, such as suicide and mental breakdown, to social conditions and location or about treating some disruptions, such as divorce and violation of certain laws, as social problems. On the other hand, such cautions have not retarded the development of an active field of social problems research in urban sociology; and in rural sociology the cautions have been put aside to some extent in recent attempts to link rapid population growth in small towns to rising rates of a wide range of social disorders (see critical reviews by Baldassare, 1981; and Wilkinson et al., 1982). A more likely reason for the absence of a sustained body of research on social disruptions in rural sociology is the enduring assumption that the quality of social life simply is better in more rural areas than in more urbanized areas, notwithstanding rural deficits in jobs and income, services, and equality.

There has been a tendency in rural sociology since its origins early in the twentieth century to assume that the effects of isolation and austerity in rural areas are counter-balanced by cohesion and mutual support in rural families and communities. Pitirim Sorokin (1929) used this argument to explain differences in suicide rates between rural and urban areas. Essays by Georg Simmel (1950) and Louis Wirth (1938) solidified a conceptual framework that attributes social pathology to the scale and complexity of city life and harmonious community functioning to the peaceful simplicity of country life. When exceptions have been found, such as a higher rural than urban rate of suicide in some areas (Schroeder and Beegle, 1953), the tendency has been to locate the cause in the spread of urban influence from the city into the surrounding countryside. This explanation protects and preserves the paradigm that assigns social problems to the city and cohesion to the rural community.

Slowly, however, evidence has been mounting to challenge this viewpoint. A review by Claude Fischer (1976:164-169) challenges the argument that urbanism breeds social problems. As he shows, the available evidence is inadequate to support such a conclusion. A review by the National Institute of Mental Health (Flax et al., 1979) challenges the assumption that psychopathology occurs at a higher rate in cities than in more rural settings. Cautiously, in light of ambiguous findings and unresolved measurement and analysis issues in the research to date, the review concludes that the weight of the evidence shows the opposite of what is widely assumed. That is, it shows a tendency for mental problems to increase in more rural settings. As Morton Wagenfeld (1982:42) observes, there is a persuasive amount of evidence in recent research on community mental health "that the halcyon picture of country life is, if not manifestly incorrect, at least open to some serious challenges." Recent studies of suicide for the United States (Stack, 1982:52) show a higher rural than urban rate, in contrast to a higher urban rate early in the twentieth century, and a pattern of only slight rural–urban differences in the 1960s. Moreover, multiple regression evidence for counties in the Northeast shows a strong positive association between the suicide rate and rural population dispersion, with other correlates of suicide controlled (Wilkinson and Israel, 1984). Similarly, results of a canonical correlation analysis for counties in the same region show a significant general pattern in which the combination of poverty and rural dispersion is associated with high rates of homicide, suicide, and divorce (Wilkinson, 1984b). Obviously much work will be needed to specify and interpret these relationships precisely; but for now it can be concluded safely that the old view of urban problems and rural harmony is largely inaccurate. Moreover, it can be argued persuasively if not yet conclusively that at least some forms of social disruption tend to be more prevalent in rural than in urban areas.

   The importance of specifying the form of disruption should be obvious from criticisms of the general disruption hypothesis in social disorganization research. This general hypothesis, as Walter Martin (1968) shows, ignores the fact that rates of some problems tend to vary negatively with one another. The available evidence, moreover, indicates that rural population dispersion has a positive association with homicide but a negative association with other violent crimes (Wilkinson, 1984b). Also, there is good reason to expect that the rate of property crime, which obviously could vary positively with the availability of property, would be greater in urban areas than in rural areas. The task of specifying the kinds of disruptions likely to be associated with rural–urban variation is a formidable one for theory and research, and this is a research challenge only recently taken up in rural sociology.

A promising theoretical lead for meeting this challenge is in the idea that ruralness affects opportunities for particular kinds of social contacts, which in turn could precipitate or discourage particular kinds of interpersonal events, including certain social disruptions. As Bruce Mayhew and Roger Levinger (1976) show, gross opportunities for contact (and disruption) vary with the number of persons in a locality. This idea can be extended to take account of evidence that different forms of disruption tend to occur in different types of contacts. Most violent crimes other than homicide occur in "nonintimate" relationships such as in contacts between strangers (Bureau of Justice Statistics, 1980:43). Homicides, on the other hand, tend to occur in more intimate relationships (Bureau of Justice Statistics, 1980:3). Similarly, studies of suicide often implicate individual isolation from intimate contacts as a key etiological factor (Trout, 1980), and family isolation from community and agency contacts is a common thread among current theoretical explanations of child abuse and neglect (Garbarino, 1980). These and other general tendencies suggest that a classification could be constructed of the kinds of contact that usually precipitate different disruptions, or for that matter a classification of contacts that usually precipitate a wide range of other events in local social life. With such a classification in hand, research could then focus on opportunities for the specified contacts to occur as these opportunities are presented and limited by locality characteristics such as rural population dispersion.

Mark Granovetter's (1973) distinction between weak ties and strong ties, mentioned earlier in this analysis as a useful device for examining the potential for community stability in different localities, offers one approach to classifying relationships that could influence social well-being. Weak ties are the kinds of contacts among strangers in which, for example, acts of nonlethal violence are more likely to occur than in other kinds of contacts, as mentioned above. Strong ties give what Durkheim (1951:356) refers to as favorable conditions for "the development of the specifically homicidal passions." The probabilities of weak ties and strong ties in a population, therefore, could affect the rates of nonlethal violence and homicide, although, of course, many other factors also could affect these rates.

Pitirim Sorokin and Carle Zimmerman's classic analysis of rural and urban "worlds" (1929:13-58) recognizes that "face to face relations occupy a less proportion of the whole interaction system of an urbanite than of a rural individual" (1929:51) and that "the totality of relations which compose the network of the interaction system of an urban individual, the part composed of casual, superficial, and short-lived relations, in contrast to permanent, strong, and durable relations, occupies a much more conspicuous place than in the interaction system of a rural dweller" (1929:53). In other words, rural–urban variation affects the probability distributions of what Granovetter calls strong and weak ties.

The thing about ruralness that affects these distributions is not culture, but distance. As ruralness increases, average distance between population units also tends to increase. The overall effect of distance is to reduce the probability of contact between any pair of units, not withstanding the availability of space-shrinking contact technologies (such as telephones) in modern society. This means rurality reduces the probability of contact—an ominous consequence for community stability as noted above but also a condition affecting the distribution of weak and strong ties.

The reduction in contacts as a consequence of rurality is likely to occur mainly in weak ties rather than in both weak and strong ties. The reason is not so much because rural people prefer strong ties, as some have assumed, but because a rural settlement pattern restricts the presence of strangers or near strangers with whom to interact. Available contacts tend to be repeated and thus become strong ties. Indeed, there appears to be no shortage of strong ties associated with ruralness but a decided shortage—a deficit from the interactional perspective on the community—of weak ties.

This hypothetical effect of ruralness on the distribution of opportunities for contacts could influence local rates of extreme and unusual events such as homicide, suicide, divorce, and nonlethal violence (Wilkinson, 1984b), but such effects are only illustrative of a much broader field of events that could be affected. Granovetter's (1973) own analysis, for example, is not concerned with such disruptions or with community action potentials (nor, one should add, with rural life) but with social mobility: the "strength" of weak ties, he argues, is in the channels they provide for upward mobility for lower-class individuals. If rural life depresses weak ties as argued, then rural life also can be identified as a constraint to upward mobility and to reducing inequality, which clearly is a stumbling block for community development.

Thus, rural life poses a number of problems of social well-being. When viewed in national perspective, the most visible of these problems are deficits in jobs and income, inadequate and missing services, and inequality of access to available resources for meeting needs. These are problems on their own, but they also contribute to a cluster of social problems related to the kinds of contacts likely to occur among people.

The heart of the problem of ruralness is to be found in what all of these other problems imply about local interaction. They suggest that ruralness restricts and, to some extent, distorts community interactions. It does this by restricting the development and maintenance of a complete and integral local society and by blocking the emergence of the community field. Previously ignored rural problems such as homicide and suicide need to be understood and addressed; but in a larger sense the relatively high rural rates of these extreme events are only symptoms of a more fundamental problem. Community is what is really at stake in the changing American countryside, and community development is what is needed for the future.

4

Rural Community Development

Rural community development has been prescribed time and again as an appropriate response to rural problems, but exactly what rural community development would entail and what it could accomplish are clouded by the variety of perspectives from which the community and development are viewed in rural sociology (Cary, 1970; Christenson and Robinson, 1989; Sanders, 1958; Summers, 1986). This chapter applies the interactional framework of the study to the questions of what community development is and how it can be encouraged as a means of improving rural well-being. These are academic questions, and the analysis approaches them primarily as such; but they relate as well to ideological and practical issues that cannot be ignored in pursuing the applied mission of rural sociology. Concepts in this analysis can serve as guides for both understanding and practice.

THE PROCESS OF COMMUNITY DEVELOPMENT

The interactional theory of community uses the concept of the community field (see Wilkinson, 1970b) to denote the network of social interactions that contains and integrates various community interests in a local society. Community development can be viewed, therefore, as a process of developing the community field (see Wilkinson, 1972). The community field, as discussed in

Chapter 1, represents the capacity of local residents to work together for their own well-being, and community development builds that capacity. In spelling out the interactional concept of community development, therefore, the first step is to review the notion of the community as a social field.

A community field, to begin with, is a social field—a process of social interaction. As in most uses by sociologists, a social field is viewed as a kind of social whole (Mey, 1972), but as one without boundaries or other fixed characteristics. A social field is an unbounded whole, an emergent structure in a dynamic process of social action (Wilkinson, 1970b; Yinger, 1965). It is said to be unbounded because its constituent elements are the acts of people and not the physical or definitional phenomena that generally are taken to be the referents of the term "boundary." An act can be in several fields of interaction simultaneously, and the fields, therefore, overlap and shade into one another. Core, interactional properties of the field, rather than boundaries, give it the quality of being an integral whole.

As a whole, the social field differs from the sum of its elements; and the difference, as in any whole (or system) is due to part–whole integration (Holzner, 1967). The social field, although unbounded, emerges in social interactions as the acts of people come to be interrelated. The whole formed by these interrelated acts then becomes an influence on subsequent acts. This idea of a field as an emergent whole that influences its components has been used in many scientific disciplines to focus attention on dynamic interaction processes.

As a dynamic process, a social field is a sequence of acts displaying unity through time, and this process has constantly changing elements and structure. The process includes actors, associations, and activities. The interactions in a process have unity by virtue of the interconnections among the acts of various actors. These interconnections occur as the acts express shared interests. This obviously is a tenuous unity, however; it is tenuous because of the emergent, dynamic and boundless qualities of an interaction field. Given the vast array of forces that can affect the flow of social interaction, one can never know exactly what will happen next as the field moves from one state of unity to another. Individuals and groups, asserting private and shared purposes, can attempt with varying degrees of success to direct the flow of the process in a particular direction, but their control is never complete. Interaction inevitably brings novelty to the process.

Taking the above as a general understanding of how social interaction occurs in processes, one can delineate a number of distinctive social fields in the local society. In many localities, for example, one finds evidence of a field of more or less related activities expressing an interest in local economic development. This field, like others, consists of acts by different people and in various groups, occurring perhaps over an extended period of time and sometimes with little apparent organization or planning. The sum of the acts nonetheless can be seen in some localities to comprise a social whole, albeit a whole with dynamic and changing features. Similarly, analysis often discovers a local social field concerned with services and others concerned with other particular interests that local residents have in common.

Among the many fields one might find in a local society, each with its actors, associations, activities, and interests, some obviously are more locality-oriented than others (see Sutton and Kolaja, 1960a, 1960b; Wilkinson, 1970a). Those that are highly oriented to the locality are the ones that have principal actors who are local residents, and the goals or interests of the actions in such fields are clearly identified with the locality. Moreover, locality-oriented actions tend to serve public rather than private interests. Locality orientation is the hallmark of community action (Wilkinson, 1970a).

Community actions (i.e., actions with considerable locality orientation) occur in social fields. For purposes of analysis one can distinguish among these fields according to the interests they pursue, although without any real boundaries among fields, it is often difficult to draw such distinctions with precision. Still, it is usually possible to identify at least general categories such as economic development, service development, environmental protection, and so on. Distinctions among different fields of community action are especially important for locating what Frederick Bates and Lloyd Bacon (1972) call "interstitial" systems—those that link the various components of a community into a whole. From the interactional perspective, the mechanism that links the various fields of community action in the local society, and the central object of the study and practice of community development, is the community field.

The community field, a special field among other fields of community action, pursues not any single interest, as most other fields may be said to do, but the general community interest instead. The actions in this field serve to coordinate other action fields, organizing them more or less (through an unbounded, dynamic, and emergent process) into a whole. The community field has actors, associations, and activities, as any social field does; but the interest that guides this field is an interest in structure rather than in specific goals such as economic development or service improvement. The structural interest in the community field is expressed through linking, coordinating actions, actions that identify and reinforce the commonality that permeates the differentiated special interest fields in a community.

In a sense, the community field is both a consequence and a cause of community actions in special interest areas. It arises from the other actions and fields, drawing together their commonalities. Having emerged, it influences subsequent actions, reinforcing the holistic structure of community that exists among them. Thus, the community field is an abstraction from other fields of community action, and its contribution is that of articulating and enforcing linkages among the other fields.

Linking, coordinating activities in the community field, can be described as a process of generalization across interest lines. Generalization organizes the common elements of locality orientation in various interest fields and gives structure to the whole of the community as an interactional phenomenon. This process of generalization occurs through acts of individuals, which can be called community leadership roles (Kaufman and Wilkinson,

1967), and through activities in informal networks and in formal coordinating associations. As is true in any social field, the process of interaction that drives and constitutes the community field is in a continuous process of change and development. Thus, the structure of the community field is never fixed; it exists in the ebb and flow of the process of generalization, which in turn arises and is constantly modified by locality-oriented actions in special interest fields. Development of this process is the central activity in community development.

Development, from the interactional viewpoint, is more than an undirected or mechanical process of change. From other perspectives, development might be seen either as an accidental or random process over which local people have essentially no control or as the natural unfolding and maturation of a differentiated structure from its embryonic form. Certainly, from the interactional perspective, as from any other, chance and natural evolution must be recognized as powerful forces in community change; but these are not what is meant by community development. Community development refers to *purposive* efforts to build the generalized structure that characterizes a community field. People try to build the community field, and the process of trying constitutes community development.

Purpose in this conception must face, of course, an unstable, essentially unpredictable social reality. Order and unity are always in question in an interaction process, and purpose represents an attempt to impose order and to create unity. Standing against the purpose of building a community field, moreover, are the purposes of individuals and groups who pursue private interests in the local arena. The interactional theory postulates no systemic or organic force to assure order, continuity, or balance in this turbulent setting. Still, problems arise and people address them purposively and sometimes collectively on behalf of the community as a whole. Through purposive attempts to articulate and strengthen a community field, local actors try to give unity and meaning to the social life they share in the locality. These attempts, expressing shared purpose, comprise the process of development.

Community change, of course, is a broad and complex process that cannot be guided entirely by any single force, such as human will, and certainly not entirely by the will to develop community as an interactional structure. By the same token, however, when community interaction is viewed as a dynamic and emergent process rather than as one determined in its course by natural laws or universal principles of order, the potential influence of the imposition of human purpose into that process cannot be dismissed as a force. Purpose is likely to have some effect, if not to control entirely the course of community change. Development, as that term is used here, means that purpose is imposed into the turbulence of dynamic social fields, and the imposition of this force gives at least some degree of order and unity to those fields.

Community change, therefore, is a broader and more complicated process than community development, although community development can be a factor in community change. At least occasionally, in the matrix of forces in change, the efforts of people to build and protect some valued or otherwise important structure among themselves comes into play. Community development occurs when people attempt purposively to increase or to reinforce the generality of interactional relationships among their various fields of locality-oriented action.

Thus, community development, when it occurs, is one part of the larger process of community change. Ecological, organizational, situational, and other forces converge to structure and alter the relationships among people in a local setting, and random events also bring turbulence to the local arena. Given this, it would be an error to say that "the community acts" in any literal sense, even in situations where community actions might occur. Instead, people act, and their actions connect with the acts of others to form action fields. Similarly, one cannot expect purposive action alone to transform a turbulent arena into a solid community. Nonetheless, given the latent potential for community to emerge among people who live together in a locality, as described in previous chapters, there remains in almost any setting the possibility that community development will occur.

Even in the most dynamic of local settings, there occasionally appears a process in which local actors attempt consciously to create or strengthen the networks through which they can work together to solve their community problems and express their shared interests in the locality. When this occurs it is community development, whatever might be its prospects of actually bringing about the intended changes. It is purposive, structure-building action in the community field, and as such it can play an important role in the social well-being of community residents, as discussed in Chapter 3. To understand this role, it is important to have a clear picture of certain qualities attributed to community development by this concept.

First, this concept of community development specifies purposive action. Community development is always purposive. To be sure, unintentional actions and purposive actions other than community development can influence community interactions, and these must be taken into account in assessing the effects of community development. Community development, however, as an expression of a particular purpose, has distinctive origins and is likely, therefore, to have distinctive effects—effects that cannot be understood apart from an understanding of the elemental bond of interaction among people who live together. This bond produces the purpose that becomes community development.

Second, community development expresses a purpose that always is positive. Taking a relativistic stance, "positive" means simply that the purpose expresses what the actors believe to be a way of improving their lives. Given, however, that the purpose in this case is to develop a particular form of social organization, namely, a community field, and given the assumption that development of this form of social organization tends to enhance social well-being, a somewhat stronger statement can be made than would be appropriate from a strictly relativistic stance. The argument here is not simply that community development is positive because people *think* it will improve their lives; the argument is that community development is positive because it in fact contributes to social well-being. The purposive action in community development can be judged to be positive not only on the basis of subjective values but also on the basis of objective conditions and consequences.

Third, a most important qualification is that community development as a purposive and positive process exists in the efforts of people and not necessarily in goal achievement. Trying is enough to qualify as community development by this concept. To require "success" as a condition would be to ignore the complex forces other than purpose that contribute to community change, and such a requirement would miss the point that development is a process rather than an outcome of social interaction. Trying, in itself, is rare in many local settlements. Development exists simply in the action that is undertaken with positive purpose. Whether or not the positive purposes of the actors are seen by the actors themselves or by others as having been achieved, development occurs to the extent the action occurs. This is the case because, in interactional terms, action is what produces structure, and not the opposite. The very fact of purposive action itself articulates the linkages that comprise the structure of a community field.

Fourth, therefore, community development is structure oriented. Harold Kaufman (1959) makes this point when he distinguishes between development *in* the community and development *of* the community. As Gene Summers (1986) maintains, both forms of development can affect the well-being of a local population. Only the latter, however, is structure oriented. Only the process of attempting to build the structure of the community field qualifies explicitly as community development. An important consideration for policy and practice, as will become apparent in the following discussion of community development in rural America, is to understand the effects of development *in* the community on development *of* the community.

Before discussing those effects, implications of the concept of purpose need to be elaborated. The concept of an orientation to structure is central to the notion that community development is purposive action, and this concept therefore deserves careful consideration in theory and research. All actions, of course, can be said to have implications for task accomplishment and for the structure of relationships among actors in a process. These implications, however, are not the issue. What is important to defining community development is the orientation (i.e., the substance of the purposes) of the actors. The actors usually have specific tasks and goals in mind, and they tend to give little thought to the structure of relationships through which the goals are pursued. Community development occurs, if at all, when the actors attend explicitly to the relationships among themselves and try in some way to alter those relationships, specifically so as to increase the generality of the relationships among themselves. This orientation of the actors to the structure of community relationships is a most distinctive property of community development.

Structure orientation also is the central quality of what can be called community leadership. Daniel Katz and Robert Kahn (1966) make a similar point in defining organizational leadership. The influence of an organizational leader, they say, transcends routine performance of assigned roles and routine exercise of the authority attached to positions. The organizational leader goes beyond routine and authority to influence changes in the structure of the organization. In their view, the leader operates within the rules of a system but acts purposively to change the structure so as to "improve" the system. Similarly, in articulating a concept of community leadership, the emphasis must be on acts that go beyond routine performance of prescribed roles. Community leadership involves, as its essential feature, an orientation of an actor to the process of building the structure of the community field.

Taking influence as a defining characteristic of leadership (Wilkinson, 1970a), one might identify many leadership roles in community actions. Only some of these, however, would qualify clearly as community leadership roles by the definition used here.

An actor might lead a specific community project, for example, but have little if any interest or involvement in the process of attempting to build community structure. Would such an actor, then, be a community leader? While a simple yes or no answer would ignore the fact that all purposive actions to improve the common life of local residents can have at least some effects on community structure, the criterion would be that community leadership occurs in such actions only to the extent that the actors attend consciously to matters of community structure.

A continuum or hierarchy can be suggested rather than a simple dichotomy. Generalized, structure-oriented behavior is more clearly community leadership than is highly specialized task-oriented leadership, although both can contribute to community development. In practical terms, the issue in point is simply one of the extent to which an actor considers and seeks to serve the community, as it were, while pursuing some more specific action objective. To the extent that this happens, it is community development, and the actor plays a community leadership role.

While the study of leadership at the individual level is of obvious importance in the study of community development, an appreciation of the substance and consequences of leadership behaviors should depend mainly on an understanding of the sociological process within which those behaviors have meaning and influence. Task orientation and structure orientation at the individual level relate at the sociological level to a distinction between two aspects of the process of community development.

Various models of community action in the sociological literature distinguish between these two aspects or dimensions of the process, referring to one typically as task accomplishment and to the other as structure maintenance. The former moves toward a specific goal, and the latter builds community relationships. Much attention has been given in the literature to the task accomplishment dimension, particularly to the delineation of the component phases or stages of the process of seeking or achieving some specific goal. Less attention has been given to the crucial but necessarily more abstract analysis of the structure-building dimension of community action. Without structure building, task accomplishment is likely to be transitory at best.

Studies of the makeup of specific task accomplishment processes sometimes identify a number of episodes addressing different issues (see Kaufman, 1959). Frequently, these episodes are posed in theory as a more or less orderly sequence of stages, but research on them reveals that the orderly arrangement occurs more in the minds of observers than in the interaction processes themselves (Wilkinson, 1970a). Using the interactional approach, it is more appropriate to view the component episodes of an action process as phases that might occur in any sequence or even simultaneously. They simply are acts that respond to action problems, and they occur as the problems arise at some point in the process of action.

Typically, as numerous studies in rural sociology have shown, task accomplishment has five phases, each addressing a distinctive action problem (Wilkinson, 1970a). *Initiation and spread of interest* addresses the issue of "awareness," as people recognize or define some issue as a problem or opportunity and begin to discuss it as a potential focus for group action. *Organization of sponsorship* addresses the issue of organization, as interested parties form some structure—a committee, a new group, an adaptation of an existing group, or some other unit—to deal with the problem. The issue of "decision-making" stimulates a phase of *goal-setting and strategy formulation*, as actors select targets for action and develop a plan for reaching those targets. A phase of *recruitment* addresses the issue of "resource mobilization," as the actors seek to secure the resources that will be needed, such as participants, goodwill, authorization, and money, to achieve the action goals. An *implementation* phase, addressing the issue of "resource application," brings the resources to bear on the action goals. One important use of such a phase model has been to delineate specific leadership roles in community actions (Beaulieu and Ryan, 1984).

Considering the structure-building dimension of community interaction (see Wilkinson, 1974), the same action issues identified in studies of task accomplishment can be used to identify the activities that explicitly articulate the structure of the community field. "Awareness" at the more generalized structural level entails planning and evaluation across interest lines—a process of building widespread consciousness of linkages among various fields of interest. The issue of "organization" at this level is manifested in attempts to coordinate and integrate actions in various fields; actors address this issue by forming multi-interest networks and organizations and by creating interorganizational linkages to assure continued contact across interest lines and beyond the course of any single project. "Decision-making" as a structure-building activity in the community field means developing long-range goals and programs to pursue multiple community interests through coordinated actions; leaders in this phase articulate a meta-image or vision of what they want the community to become in the future as a result of their concerted local actions. In "resource mobilization" the activities include legitimizing groups to coordinate actions, building cohesion, developing new leaders and leadership skills, and encouraging participation in community planning and development. "Resource application" as a process of building community structure means using resources judiciously and selectively in given projects with an eye to the needs of other projects and to future demands on local resources. Actors play these roles in the process of building and maintaining the structure of the community field just as they play specific phase roles in given action projects. Community development occurs as the actors in task accomplishment episodes give attention to these generalizing activities.

RURAL COMMUNITY DEVELOPMENT IN AMERICA

With this discussion of the process of community development as one part of the background, and with the characteristics of rural areas and populations as another part (from the discussion in Chapter 2), the question now to be addressed is a central one of this study, namely: How can rural community development be encouraged? This is both a theoretical issue in the sociology of community and a practical challenge for applied rural sociology. Many factors obviously would be involved in answering such a question, but the preceding discussions provide at least some general guidelines. For one, it is clear that if community development is essentially a structure-building activity as argued here, efforts to promote that activity through policy, education, or other mechanisms must address structural issues and must not rest entirely on attempts to change either material conditions or individual orientations and skills. Secondly, any attempt to promote community development in local areas must recognize that many of the problems to be overcome in achieving such a goal are affected by nonlocal factors. Thirdly, a realistic appraisal of the prospects for community development in rural areas can help to form an agenda for action. In particular, such an appraisal can help to specify the constraints to be faced and the resources available for promoting rural well-being through community development. These guidelines give a general strategy for studying and encouraging rural community development.

A structural approach is needed both because the process of community development itself is one of building structure and because the principal constraints to community development in rural America are structural in nature. On the one hand, a structural approach is needed to complement the individual-level approach of many leadership education programs. The latter clearly can have merit, but taken alone efforts to impart knowledge, skill, and confidence to potential leaders can miss the mark of what is needed for community development. Leadership education programs might contribute more to individual development than to community development unless those programs are designed to focus directly on building the skills needed to build community structure. Such a focus is necessary to avoid the tendency for individual efforts in the community to become self-seeking and fragmented rather than community-building and coordinated. Moreover, any program that rests entirely on changing the minds and attitudes of individuals as a strategy of improving social well-being carries the implicit threat of "blaming the victims" (see Ryan, 1971) of larger structural causes of the problems individuals face. Education for community development has an important contribution to make, but to be effective in building community structure and enhancing social well-being, education of individuals must be coupled with other efforts to attack the structural sources of rural problems.

Likewise, a useful approach to rural community development must go beyond a grassroots strategy. Without denying that community development is a process of local action, one also must recognize that this process in rural areas often is constrained more by factors at regional, national, and international levels than by factors at the local level. Expecting the rural community to solve its own problems without changing the larger society "blames the victims" in its own way.

An effective strategy must address rural constraints to community development while retaining and building upon whatever advantages rural areas might have for community development. How can this be done? As noted earlier, rural localities generally need more jobs and income, better services, and other aspects of increased access to resources for meeting daily needs. Increasing access to these resources can serve as a foundation for community interaction to emerge and persist in the local society. In many cases, however, access to the needed resources depends on factors beyond the control of local actors. Consequently, if a development program depends for its success only on the efforts of local actors, it cannot be expected to overcome some of the most serious constraints to development in rural areas.

In recent years, many of the most significant changes in rural America have been due to largely unplanned shifts in national and international economies, such as changing energy markets and agricultural trade patterns and the shift from manufacturing to services as the dominant growth sector of the economy. By and large these shifts reflect efforts by large organizations and other actors in worldwide systems to pursue their own interests. Few if any large-scale changes have occurred in these systems explicitly for the purpose of serving the needs of rural residents. Thus, even though some growth has occurred in rural areas, the forces behind the growth tend not to be oriented toward increasing rural welfare (see Till, 1981). Unplanned rural development holds little promise of either supporting sustained growth in rural population and employment or of encouraging community development.

What would be the key to increasing the availability of resources to meet the needs of people in rural areas and thus to increasing the possibility that community could develop and be sustained in rural settings? As things stand, rural deficits in resources for meeting needs are a powerful barrier to community development and well-being. One proposal might be to alter the national pattern of spatial inequality so as to make ruralness less of a disadvantage, although that would require intervention to confront vested interests (see Lovejoy and Krannich, 1982). While some reforms in the national pattern no doubt could be made if there were a national will to change them, the constituency of rural advocates pushing for such reforms appears to be too small and too poorly organized to have anything more than modest occasional effects. Ruralness seems likely to continue to be a source of disadvantage in access to jobs, income, services, and many other goals in the future as it has been in the past, notwithstanding periods of rural growth and notwithstanding developments in technology that could, in theory, overcome the "friction of rural space" (see Dillman, 1985). Programs to implement these developments too often express the interests of actors outside rural areas who benefit indirectly and implicitly, if not directly and explicitly, from the patterns of spatial inequality that sustain rural disadvantages. Thus, long-term effects of rural growth and new technology on the relative well-being of rural populations are not likely to be positive without policy actions to make sure that these effects are positive.

If ruralness is likely to continue to be a source of disadvantages, an alternative way to promote rural well-being in some areas would be to reduce the extent of ruralness in local populations. Growth in jobs, income, services, and access to other means of meeting local needs occurs primarily through urbanization of rural areas. This appears to be one of the factors having substantial effects on the well-being of people in rural areas today (see Hawley, 1978). The apparent reason, from the perspective of this study, is that urbanization, up to some threshold point (see Hock, 1976), increases adaptive capacity of a local population, and this can make rural areas less dependent on larger centers, less isolated from vital resources, and more capable of maintaining a complete local society. Other things being equal, growth in a rural area allows the local society to become more comprehensive, and this increases the possibility for community to emerge in the local society.

Other things rarely are equal, of course, and qualifications about the characteristics of the growth process must be considered. For one thing, a strategy of meeting rural needs through urban growth can only benefit rural areas that have growth potential or that have the potential to become part of a viable rural–urban growth field. For another, problems of coping with growth can be as distressing in rural areas as problems of coping with the absence of growth. Moreover, growth promotion in rural areas has a spotty record, at best, as a strategy of increasing local well-being (Wilkinson, 1989). Findings by Craig Humphrey and Richard Krannich (1980), for example, show that local growth promotion tends to be more of a consequence than a cause of growth. Local leaders often seek to respond to problems associated with decline by promoting growth. This relationship can be understood in light of the general finding in community action research that "problems" tend to be among the best predictors of local mobilization (see Wilkinson et al., 1984). Furthermore, even in studies that show positive effects of mobilization on achievement of widely endorsed local goals, the effects of mobilization tend to be modest relative to the effects of other variables (e.g., Lloyd and Wilkinson, 1985; Luloff and Wilkinson, 1979; Martin and Wilkinson, 1984). Growth promotion also is made suspect as a development strategy by the charge that this activity tends to express elite interests rather than the interests of the community as a whole (Molotch, 1976).

To be sure, local growth promotion, under certain conditions, can contribute to community development. Without changes on other variables, however, the positive effect of simply trying to improve the community can be overwhelmed by the effects of powerful barriers in rural areas to achieving this goal. In such cases, the efforts of the actors are likely to diminish.

It is necessary, therefore, that rural growth be promoted at state, regional, and national levels to help build an environment in which local efforts can have some hope of success. Without hope of success in achieving local action goals, local motivation for action is likely to flag.

At state, regional, and national levels, where major processes affecting rural conditions are organized, directly confronting those who have vested interests in spatial inequality is likely to be less effective than a more positive strategy of building on some of the advantages rural areas have to offer. For example, residential preferences and widely shared values in society, as shown in many surveys (see Zuiches, 1981), tend to venerate small communities. This gives something of a base of positive sentiment at the national level on which to construct and promote programs to improve rural employment opportunities, services, and so on—programs that would make it possible for more people to act on their stated preferences for living in small centers. Similarly, as Edward Blakely and Ted Bradshaw (1985) point out, the shift now occurring from a manufacturing economy to an information and service economy in the larger society means that human knowledge and skills rather than location and natural resources will dominate economic activities in the future. In such a shift, new opportunities might be found for rural areas to attract population and economic resources. In the community of the future, ties to the outside, which some observers in the past have seen as threats to the community, could become channels to important resources. In addition to these opportunities, which can be cultivated in many ways through policies and programs that do not necessarily confront dominant patterns in the American political economy, rural settlements also have certain inherent advantages for community development and these can be protected and built upon to promote local social well-being. The "human-scale" of social organization in rural areas, for example, presents a decided advantage in the process of community development, although this advantage can be suppressed if other conditions, such as access to resources, are not met. Indeed, for some communities, the attractions associated with being perceived as "rural" by prospective migrants can be stimuli to growth.

Growth alone, however, no matter how much it is needed and no matter how successful the efforts to promote it might be, gives little assurance that community development will occur in rural areas. Granted that growth often brings economic resources and services to bear on unmet local needs, to be effective in stimulating community development the growth also must occur in such a way as to have positive effects on articulating the local social relationships that constitute the essence of community development. With community development, growth can increase social well-being in rural areas. Without community development, growth can be disruptive and divisive in local social organization. It is useful, therefore, to consider how rural growth affects other factors in addition to access to needed resources.

The effect of growth on equality is crucial for reasons discussed in Chapter 3. Inequality is a barrier to the free flow of authentic interaction among people whose lives are interconnected in a local society, and community development depends upon—indeed, occurs within—an unrestrained process of social interaction. If growth increases inequality, as certainly is possible if not inevitable, it can stifle and distort the contacts among people that are necessary for community development. This particularly is a threat when growth serves the interest of an elite group rather than that of the community as a whole. The opposite can occur when growth in a small community upsets an existing structure of inequality, making it possible for interaction to occur where it was blocked before. Community development in such a case is encouraged by increased interaction even if the increase carries heightened potential for conflict. The effect of growth on interaction by virtue of its effect on equality, therefore, is an important qualification to the assertion that growth can promote community development in rural areas.

Another qualification is the effect of growth on community action. Community development, as discussed in this study, can occur only where there is community action. Growth, in turn, can contribute to community development only by contributing to community action. The resources and problems associated with growth can set the stage for community action, but growth also can block it. Cases of the latter abound in the literature on small communities (e.g., Bridger, 1988). In some instances, growth, stimulated by outside forces and organization, bypasses local action processes entirely. In other cases, organizations and individuals work to prevent local action from occurring (see, for example, Wilkinson, 1969) so as to minimize interference with growth promotion. Growth likewise can produce opportunities that divert community leaders into schemes to enhance their own welfare, and it can produce and uncover cleavages in the community that are barriers to community development. While much is yet to be learned about the effects of growth on community interaction, at least one strategic principle can be drawn from the theoretical perspective of this study. If growth is to be an effective means of promoting community development in rural areas, provision must be made for the growth to involve and encourage community action. Community development occurs only in community action.

The conditions discussed above as targets or goals of policy and education can be said to prepare the ground for community development to occur. Growth, for those communities with growth potential, can help to fill gaps in the local society by bringing jobs, income, services, and other resources to meet the needs of local residents. With these resources in hand, the local society can have a complete structure of institutions, groups and activities. The common life among people in this structure can then serve as a base for interactions to produce the phenomenon of community among them. Where the growth encourages equality it facilitates open, authentic interaction processes through which people in the local society create and discover the bond of community. Where the local society is a whole and the interaction is not repressed or perverted by cleavages, community actions— collective efforts to improve the shared conditions of local life—tend to occur; and community actions are the processes from which the community field emerges. Under the right conditions, community development occurs not so much because of the efforts of teachers or outside "developers," but simply because community development is what happens among people when the conditions are right. They tend to work together to build community relationships among themselves. Unfortunately, however, many rural localities have little growth potential.

In a nutshell, the key to policy and practice of community development is to attack the barriers to a natural process. When the effects of the barriers are muted, community development takes care of itself as the people go about the natural process of living together as a community. If the barriers persist, however, this process is blocked. And that, in a nutshell, is the prevailing situation in much of rural America.

The solution, if there is one, is purposive intervention. Purposive collective action is needed to increase rural economic resources, improve rural services, reduce inequality, and facilitate local leadership in planning and decision-making about community changes. Policy interventions will be needed at all levels of government to protect rural interests. Interventions in science and education will be needed to support and guide the efforts of actors at all levels. Intervention at the local level, of course, is the essence of the process of community development, but this can only succeed in rural areas if actors at other levels work to clear the way for it to succeed.

There is contemporary evidence of a rural development policy movement at the federal level in the United States (Wilkinson, 1986b), but since this movement began in the late 1960s its theme has been restricted primarily to rural economic development. In one sense, this is as it should be given the severity of rural economic problems and the devastating effects of these problems on the probability of rural community development. Economic development, however, does not contribute automatically to community development and, in fact, can prevent or disrupt community development unless there is purposive intervention to make community development its explicit goal and rationale. So far in the contemporary rural development policy movement, community development has not been an explicit goal; as a consequence, the rural economic development that has occurred has not contributed substantially to rural community development. Communities, by and large, have not been actively involved, and without community involvement there can be no community development. What is needed, therefore, following the hypothesis put forward in this analysis, is a policy of rural development that explicitly is a policy of rural community development. The policy goal should be to assist local actors in developing the capacity to solve local problems.

Rural economic development must continue to be the task of first priority in a policy to promote rural well-being, but to be successful this task must have community development as its rationale and goal. Economic development for community development has distinctive characteristics that economic development alone might not have. It seeks to increase the base of resources for rural people to meet their needs. It encourages the development of services, groups, and facilities that are needed for a complete local society. It seeks to reduce inequality. It provides for and depends upon local community action and involvement. If it would do all this, then rural economic development could contribute directly to rural social well-being both by providing jobs and income and by encouraging community development.

5

In Search of the Community in the Changing Countryside

The interactional approach gives a framework for relating the concepts of community and rural to social well-being and a general strategy for attacking rural problems through community development. This chapter draws together the various parts of the argument that has been used to organize a review of critical issues in the rural sociological literature and highlights their implications for future work in the field.

THE INTERACTIONAL COMMUNITY

The idea that the community is an interactional phenomenon gives a distinctive way of thinking about social life and social well-being in rural areas. Sociology, of course, always has been interested in social interaction, but only recently has this interest become an organizing focus for theories of community and social structure. For many years in sociology, the community was received mainly as an ecological unit, rural as a particular cultural form and development mainly as the evolution of modern social systems. Today these conventional views are disputed, and some critics even argue for discarding the concepts—community, rural, and development—to which they refer. The interactional viewpoint, in contrast, recasts the old concepts as tools for understanding critical issues in the well-being of people.

What is the community and what does it do for people? How does rural location affect the community and social well-being? How can community development and well-being be encouraged in rural areas? These questions about local social interaction have organized the framework of this study. As has been maintained throughout this discussion, the interactional community has three essential properties, and these provide criteria for assessing the extent of community in a population settlement. First, as conventional approaches insist, the community is a local ecology, meaning an organization of social life for meeting daily needs and adapting to changes in a particular territorial and social environment. Second, as an organization of social life, the community is a comprehensive interactional structure. It is a social whole, a common life that expresses not simply one need or interest but the full round of common needs and interests of local residents. It is a more or less complete common life, a holistic structure, and a complete table of organization, although, of course, the lives of people need not be wholly contained within its boundaries. Third, the community is a bond of local solidarity. This solidarity is expressed in community actions. The residents of a community live together, sharing a common life, and they also act together solving common problems and seizing opportunities for improving their common life.

The combination of these three properties—local ecology, social organization, and community action—produces a social bond that is natural and ubiquitous, whether or not it is experienced cognitively or responded to emotionally. It simply emerges unless something blocks it. As a natural state of being-in-relationship to others, it exists simply because people have natural relationships with one another and these comprise a common life. When community is experienced consciously, it can arouse feeling, and this cognitive and emotional response to the experience of community is communion. Communion celebrates community.

Community in this sense is natural in that it is not contrived. People, by the nature of being human, engage in social relationships with others on a continuing basis and they have their social being and identity in that interaction. Community, therefore, is a natural disposition among people, and anything that stands in the way of such a natural disposition is a barrier to human well-being.

Whether community is related to locality, however, has become a controversial point. One objection to a territorial definition of community, as reviewed in this study, is the observation that travel, long-distance communications, and complex organizations now link people to many localities. The importance of these linkages might be such that a given territory no longer contains the range of contacts and relationships that constitute an interactional community. At some earlier time, perhaps, community was strictly localized and human interaction was confined to a fairly small territory for most people. In contrast, many sociologists today call for a territory-free concept of the community, or at least for a concept by which the relationships define the territory and not vice versa. Outside contacts make it possible for people to belong to many communities, according to this reasoning.

While a question might be raised as to whether residential mobility has increased or decreased over the past century or so, there is little doubt that technology has increased the frequency of contact among localities. Whether this spells the end of the historical association between community and place is another question. Choice has increased, but attachment to place has not necessarily declined as a result. What has declined, as argued in this study (following Fischer, 1977), is the extent to which people are restricted to a particular place. Compared to a half century ago, fewer people now are forced to stay in a place and fewer are forced to leave. People have more choices than in the past. This marks a change in the local community but not necessarily the demise of community. The tie of community is no longer one of bondage, but it is a tie nonetheless, a bond among people who share a given place.

Other critics of the territorial concept of community take different approaches, arguing, for instance, that the nation or mass society has become the community and that community now refers to intimate networks that transcend places. Still others note that the quest for community in localities represents an attempt by elite groupings to repress or mask class conflicts.

Perhaps overall, the most telling criticism of the territorial concept of community is one based on analyses of the outside ties of the various separate components of local societies. People, groups, special interest fields, and so on—the components of a community—appear in many cases to be tied more closely to systems outside the locality than to one another. Community subsystems are said by some observers to be integrated, but the integration is into a "vertical" system or pattern in the larger society rather than into a "horizontal" system or pattern in the local society. If this observation is correct, the community is mainly a stage where essentially unconnected systems represent the outside world. The community as a whole has little integrity, it could be argued.

What can one make of these criticisms of the ideal type of the local community? Serious controversies challenge the claim that community is a locality, a local society, and a community field, as argued in this study. The boundaries of the locality overlap with those of other settlements, and they change rapidly. The local society contains units tightly linked to systems outside the locality, and the outside connections often are stronger than those within the local society. Community action is said to be depressed by the effects of urbanization and to be inconsistent with the differenti-ation and stratification of the modern locality. Why continue to search for the community within the local society if the path to social well-being now lies elsewhere?

In contrast to these criticisms, the approach of this study finds much of value in the territorial concept and much usefulness in continuing to study and promote the community as a local social field. The reasons are found in the concept of social well-being as a quality of social interaction. This concept, as developed here in interactional terms, uses the idea of lower-order and higher-order needs. When primary or lower-order needs are met to such a degree as to release energy and attention from the struggle for survival, human interest turns to creating, maintaining, and expanding social relationships with others, especially with the others with whom one lives. Community is the proximate setting for contact with society; it is the locus of the interactions that structure the self-concept and build respect for self and others; it provides opportunities for expressing needs for association and involvement; and it allows people to participate in creating their own living conditions. This study argues that community gives a focus to human action, thus reducing tendencies to degrade and destroy the ecological structures that support social life. Modern trends have not altered the essential properties of the community, nor have these trends reduced the importance of the community in social well-being. They have, however, altered the probability that community will emerge from its latent form in some localities and contribute as much as it might to social well-being. Barriers to community development are readily apparent in rural America in particular.

RURAL COMMUNITY PROBLEMS

Contrary to the conventional and now widely criticized view that rural means *Gemeinschaft* (that is, a close-knit traditional form of social life in small settlements), the interactional approach draws attention to the disadvantages rural areas have for the kinds of social interactions that produce community and support social well-being. The essential ecological meaning of rural—dispersed settlement—affects each of the three elements of the interactional concept of the community; namely, its common territory, complete local society, and field of community interactions.

Without a sufficient base of resources in the local area to meet primary needs, rural residents must do without or they must look outside the local territory for the resources they need. Findings of many studies show that rural people often travel great distances and to multiple centers to meet their needs for work, trade, education, health services, recreation, and government services. Where this occurs, contacts in rural areas tend to be disproportionately in intimate relationships or "strong ties." The reason is not that the relationships for meeting most needs are primary. The reason is simply that people leave the territory to meet many of their daily needs. Dispersion of population and small population size limit the local resource base, and the rural setting tends to lack a complete array of services and facilities. It also tends to lack the complete networks of social interaction and relationships a community would provide to meet the social needs of the people.

Thus, the locality in rural America often is a place of residence only as relatives and neighbors who are strongly tied to one another have few mutual contacts in their separate involvements outside the place of residence. In some cases, of course, outside contacts are limited for most residents, producing insularity and rural malaise. A locality must have a comprehensive local society for community to develop fully in local social interaction, and rural localities often have major parts missing in their local societies—parts such as employment, formal education, and other services and groups.

Along with a complete local society, community requires an integrated network of interactions. Perhaps in times past social cohesion in a complete network of community relations compensated for the physical isolation of the remote rural settlement. Recent evidence neither confirms nor denies this as a historical observation, but the recent findings give a very different picture of contemporary life in small, relatively isolated settlements. Studies of such problems as suicide and homicide in rural America, for example, question the notion that rates of these problems tend to increase with urbanization and suggest instead that rural life itself is disruptive and problem-ridden. Evidence also is fairly clear that local activeness, represented by community efforts to improve community conditions, tends to be less prevalent in rural than in urban areas. Apparently, rural conditions limit community development, although much more research will be needed to show exactly how and why this is so.

TOWARD RURAL COMMUNITY DEVELOPMENT

Going beyond the discussion of problems to the search for solutions, a most important starting place is the recognition that opportunities exist for rural community development, even in the turbulent environment of rural America in the 1990s. The discussion has cited residential preferences and widely-shared values in this society that continue to venerate the small-town community, thus giving in potential at least a base of positive sentiment at the national level on which to construct and support rural community development programs. Furthermore, new communications technologies—the space-shrinking technologies of the information society—could reduce the friction of rural space, making the resources of modern society available instantly to people in remote localities, although questions remain as to whether they will have this effect. Similarly, the shift from a manufacturing economy to an information and service economy means that human knowledge and skills rather than location and natural resources will be important in local economic development in the future. In the community of the future, ties to the outside might increase access to vital resources. In addition, smaller communities, by virtue of the "human-scale" of their local social organization, could have obvious advantages over larger communities for building local solidarity, other things being equal. The availability of these opportunities and advantages, however, gives no assurance that communities in rural areas will be able to use them for their own development.

Given the trends of the times in rural America, development of the small-town community will be an uphill fight (Wilkinson, 1986a). The small community needs help if community development is to occur. As a base for encouraging the latent capacity of "community" to bloom and have its beneficial effects on rural social well-being, at least four needs enumerated in this study must be addressed. First, jobs and income—good jobs and steady income—must be secured for the residents of small towns and their surrounding rural areas. Development that does not start with jobs and income simply does not start; but, by the same token, if development ends with jobs and income, it ends (Kaufman, 1985). Second, services and facilities are needed to support a complete local society in the rural locality. A complete local society is needed to serve the needs of people but also to allow the natural disposition toward community to emerge in relationships among those people. Third, inequality, a most formidable barrier to social interaction in many small communities, must be reduced to allow a true form of local solidarity to grow and to generate effective community actions. Fourth, informed and committed local leaders are needed to help accomplish these goals and to cultivate the social relationships and shared identity that are the essence of community. An agenda can be built with these goals for encouraging community development in rural America.

Rural community development will require federal actions as well as state and local action (Wilkinson, 1984a). Reducing the gap between rural and urban areas on indicators of social well-being clearly is in the general national interest. Rural initiatives are needed in virtually all major agencies of the federal government—to promote rural economic development, to improve rural services, to attack inequalities, and to stimulate community development. A concerted attack on multiple fronts is needed.

Without national leadership, the forces that have contributed to pressing rural problems will continue to restrict progress in solving those problems. State and local efforts are vital to the process of rural development, but these must be organized within a context of resolve and action at the national level. One of the most obvious facts of rural life in an essentially urban society is that many problems have their roots not in local areas but in the structure and functioning of the larger society. Rural employment, for example, is intimately connected to the national economic

structure. Rural services are affected by organizations that operate in the larger society. Rural inequalities are rooted in nation-
wide inequalities. While rural areas have special needs that
require special efforts, many of those special needs require action
at the national level.

Ultimately, however, the process of community development,
whether in small towns and rural areas or in urban centers, is a
local one. Actions and policies of federal and state agencies can
set the stage, but community development itself is an "inside job,"
a process of community-building by community actors and
groups. This view of community development as an interaction
process is summarized as follows:

> Sometimes in the configuration of ecological, cultural,
> social, psychological, and chance factors which figure in
> change in the local society, there is a category of actions
> which reflect the intentions of actors to create or strengthen
> the relationships and patterns through which they seek
> collectively to express the range of their common interests
> and to solve their community problems. It is this category
> of purposive, structure-building activities which constitutes
> community development (Wilkinson, 1972:45).

Community development, in this conception of it, is always
purposive and positive, although it may or may not be "successful" in achieving the specific goals to which it is directed.
Community "develops," as it were, in the process of action as
people work together to try to improve their lives together.

Action at either the national level or at the community level,
without the other, is likely to have far less effect on rural
well-being than would a coordinated effort involving actors at all
levels. Outside actions to promote rural economic development,
for example, without local community development, can promote
exploitation of rural resources by outside investors. By the same
token, local action to build community cohesion without attention
at other levels to the larger forces that constrain local development

can produce local frustration and bitterness. A coordinated, two-pronged attack is needed for an effective effort to allow community to flourish in rural America.

How can social well-being be achieved in rural areas? This is a question at the center of rural sociology, not simply a value issue at the political and social fringes of the discipline. Likewise, it is a question worthy of attention from the perspectives of many other disciplines. Understanding the real problems of people is the first challenge to any discipline that would seek to use science to promote social well-being. Among many problems faced by rural people in America today, this study identifies one as the central problem. Rural well-being depends on purposive actions to encourage and cultivate rural community development.

References

Aiken, Michael, and Paul E. Mott (eds.). 1970. *The Structure of Community Power.* New York: Random House.

Albrecht, Don E., and H. Reed Geertsen. 1982. "Population growth in rural communities: Residents' perceptions of its consequences." *Journal of the Community Development Society* 13(2):75–90.

Allport, Gordon. 1955. *Becoming.* New Haven, Conn.: Yale University Press.

Anderson, C. Arnold. 1959. "Trends in rural sociology." Pp. 360–75 in Robert K. Merton, Leonard Broom and Leonard S. Cottrell, Jr. (eds.), *Sociology Today: Problems and Prospects.* New York: Basic Books.

Arensberg, Conrad M. 1961. "The community as object and as sample." *American Anthropologist* 63(2):241–64.

Bachtel, Douglas C., and Joseph J. Molnar. 1980. "Black and white leader perspectives on rural industrialization." *Rural Sociology* 45(4):663–80.

Baldassare, Mark. 1981. "Local perspectives on community growth." Pp. 116–43 in Amos H. Hawley and Sara Mills Mazie (eds.), *Nonmetropolitan America in Transition.* Chapel Hill: University of North Carolina Press.

Barnes, J. A. 1954. "Class and committees in a Norwegian island parish." *Human Relations* 7(1):39–58.

Bates, Frederick L., and Lloyd Bacon. 1972. "The community as a social system." *Social Forces* 50(3):371–79.

Beaulieu, Lionel J., and Vernon D. Ryan. 1984. "Hierarchical influence structures in rural communities: A case study." *Rural Sociology* 49(1):106–16.

Bell, Colin, and Howard Newby. 1972. *Community Studies: An Introduction to the Study of the Local Community*. New York: Praeger Publishers.

Bender, Thomas. 1978. *Community and Social Change in America*. New Brunswick, N.J.: Rutgers University Press.

Benvenuti, Bruno, Benno Galjart, and Howard Newby. 1975. "The current status of rural sociology." *Sociologia Ruralis* 15(1/2):3–21.

Bernard, Jessie. 1973. *The Sociology of Community*. Glenview, Ill.: Scott, Foresman and Company.

Blakely, Edward J., and Ted K. Bradshaw. 1985. "Rural America: The community development frontier." Pp. 3–29 in Frank A. Fear and Harry K. Schwarzweller (eds.), *Focus on Community*. Volume 3 of *Research in Rural Sociology and Rural Development*. Greenwich, Conn.: JAI Press.

Bly, Carol. 1981. *Letters from the Country*. New York: Harper and Row.

Bokemeier, Janet, and John L. Tait. 1980. "Women as power actors: A comparative study of rural communities." *Rural Sociology* 45(2):238–55.

Bradley, Tony, and Philip Lowe. 1984. *Locality and Rurality: Economy and Society in Rural Regions*. Norwich, England: Geo Books.

Bridger, Jeffrey C. 1988. *The Growth Machine: A Qualitative Assessment*. Master's thesis in rural sociology. University Park.: Penn State University.

Brown, David L. 1987. *Rural Economic Development in the 1980's: A Summary*. Washington, D.C.: Economic Research Service, Agriculture Information Bulletin 533, U.S. Department of Agriculture.

Brownell, Baker. 1950. *The Human Community. Its Philosophy and Practice for a Time of Crisis*. New York: Harper & Brothers.

Brunner, Edmund DeS. 1927. *Village Communities*. New York: George H. Doran.

Brunner, Edmund DeS., Gwendolyn S. Hughes, and Marjorie Patten. 1927. *American Agricultural Villages*. New York: George H. Doran.

Brunner, Edmund DeS., and Irving Lorge. 1937. *Rural Trends in Depression Years*. New York: Columbia University Press.

Buck, Roy C. 1978. "Boundary maintenance revisited: Tourist experience in an Old Order Amish community." *Rural Sociology* 43(2):221–34.

Bureau of Justice Statistics. 1980. *Intimate Victims: A Study of Violence Among Friends and Relatives*. Washington, D.C.: U.S. Department of Justice.

Burns, Allan F. 1978. "Cargo cult in a western town: A cultural approach to episodic change." *Rural Sociology* 43(2):164–77.

Cantrell, Randolph, James Krile, and George Donohue. 1982. "The community involvement of the yoked parishes." *Rural Sociology* 47(1):81–90.

Cary, Lee J. (ed.). 1970. *Community Development as a Process.* Columbia: University of Missouri Press.

Castells, Manuel. 1977. *The Urban Question: A Marxist Approach.* Cambridge: MIT Press.

Christenson, James A., and Ronald T. Crouch. 1982. "Structural binds: Consequences for community growth." *Journal of the Community Development Society* 12(2):17–28.

Christenson, James A., and Jerry W. Robinson, Jr. (eds.). 1989. *Community Development in Perspective.* Ames: Iowa State University Press.

Christenson, James A., and Gregory S. Taylor. 1982. "Determinants, expenditures, and performance of common public services." *Rural Sociology* 47(1):147–63.

Clark, Terry N. (ed.). 1968. *Community Structure and Decision-making: Comparative Analyses.* San Francisco: Chandler.

Clinton, Charles A. 1978. "Shiloh: The little county that could—and did." *Rural Sociology* 43(2):191–203.

Colfer, Carol J. Pierce, and A. Michael Colfer. 1978. "Inside Bushler Bay: Lifeways in counterpoint." *Rural Sociology* 43(2):204–20.

Cottrell, W. F. 1951. "Death by dieselization: A case study in the reaction to technological change." *American Sociological Review* 16(3):358–65.

Craven, Paul, and Barry Wellman. 1973. "The network city." *Sociological Inquiry* 43(4):57–88.

Davis, Allison, Burleigh B. Gardner, and Mary R. Gardner. 1944. *Deep South: A Social Anthropological Study of Caste and Class.* Chicago: University of Chicago Press.

Deseran, Forrest. 1978. "Community satisfaction as definition of the situation: Some conceptual issues." *Rural Sociology* 43(2):235–49.

Dewey, Richard. 1960. "The rural–urban continuum: Real but relatively unimportant." *American Journal of Sociology* 66(1):60–66.

Dillman, Don A. 1985. "The social impacts of information technologies in rural North America." *Rural Sociology* 50(1):1–26.

Dollard, John. 1937. *Caste and Class in a Southern Town.* New Haven, Conn.: Yale University Press.

Duncan, Otis Dudley, and Albert J. Reiss, Jr. 1956. *Social Characteristics of Urban and Rural Communities, 1950.* New York: John Wiley & Sons.

Duncan, Otis Dudley, and Leo F. Schnore. 1959. "Cultural, behavioral, and ecological perspectives in the study of social organization." *American Journal of Sociology* 65(2):132–46.

Durkheim, Emile. 1933. *The Division of Labor in Society*. Translated by George Simpson. Glencoe, Ill.: The Free Press of Glencoe.

Durkheim, Emile. 1951. *Suicide*. Translated by John A. Spaulding and George Simpson. New York: The Free Press.

England, J. Lynn, and Stan L. Albrecht. 1984. "Boomtowns and social disruption." *Rural Sociology* 49(2):230–46.

Falk, William W., and Jess Gilbert. 1985. "Bringing rural sociology back in." *Rural Sociology* 50(4):561–77.

Fischer, Claude S. 1976. *The Urban Experience*. New York: Harcourt Brace Jovanovich.

Fischer, Claude S. 1977. "Comments on the history and study of 'community.'" Pp. 189–204 in Claude S. Fischer et al., *Networks and Places: Social Relations in the Urban Setting*. New York: The Free Press.

Flax, J. W., M. O. Wagenfeld, R. E. Evans, and R. J. Weiss. 1979. *Mental Health and Rural America: An Overview and Annotated Bibliography*. Washington, D.C.: Alcohol, Drug Abuse and Mental Health Administration, U.S. Public Health Service.

Ford, Thomas R., and Willis A. Sutton, Jr. 1964. "The impact of change on rural communities and fringe areas: Review of a decade's research." Pp. 198–229 in James H. Copp (ed.), *Our Changing Rural Society: Perspectives and Trends*. Ames: Iowa State University Press.

Fromm, Erich. 1947. *Man for Himself*. New York: Holt, Rinehart and Winston.

Fromm, Erich. 1956. *The Art of Loving*. New York: Harper.

Fuguitt, Glenn V. 1985. "The nonmetropolitan population turnaround." *Annual Review of Sociology* 11:259–80.

Gallaher, Art, Jr. 1961. *Plainville Fifteen Years Later*. New York: Columbia University Press.

Galpin, Charles J. 1915. *The Social Anatomy of an Agricultural Community*. Madison: University of Wisconsin Agricultural Experiment Station Bulletin 34.

Galpin, Charles J. 1918. *Rural Life*. New York: The Century Company.

Garbarino, James. 1980. *Understanding Abusive Families*. Lexington, Mass.: Lexington Books.

Garkovich, Lorraine. 1985. "Fifty-year index: volumes 1–50, 1936–1985." *Rural Sociology* 50(4):1–189.

Gaventa, John. 1980. *Power and Powerlessness: Quiescence and Rebellion in an Appalachian Valley*. Urbana, Ill.: University of Illinois Press.

Gilbert, Jess. 1982. "Rural theory: the grounding of rural sociology." *Rural Sociology* 47(4):609–33.

Goldschmidt, Walter R. 1947. *As You Sow*. New York: Harcourt, Brace.

Goodman, Paul. 1956. *Growing up Absurd: Problems of Youth in the Organized System*. New York: Random House.

Goudy, Willis J. 1977. "Evaluations of local attributes and community satisfaction in small towns." *Rural Sociology* 42(3):371–82.

Goudy, Willis J. 1983. "Desired and actual communities: Perceptions of 27 Iowa towns." *Journal of the Community Development Society* 14(1):39–49.

Goudy, Willis J., and Vernon D. Ryan. 1982. "Changing communities." Pp. 256–63 in Don A. Dillman and Daryl J. Hobbs (eds.), *Rural Society in the U.S.: Issues for the 1980s*. Boulder, Colo.: Westview Press.

Gouldner, Alvin W. 1960. "The norm of reciprocity: A preliminary statement." *American Sociological Review* 25(2):161–177.

Granovetter, Mark. 1973. "The strength of weak ties." *American Journal of Sociology* 78(6):1360–80.

Greer, Scott. 1962. *The Emerging City*. Glencoe, Ill.: The Free Press of Glencoe.

Gusfield, Joseph R. 1975. *Community: A Critical Response*. Oxford: Basil Blackwell.

Haas, David F. 1978. "Clientelism and rural development in Thailand." *Rural Sociology* 43(2):280–92.

Habermas, Jurgen. 1970. *Toward a Rational Society*. Boston: Beacon Press.

Habermas, Jurgen. 1971. *Knowledge and Human Interests*. Boston: Beacon Press.

Ham, Kum Shik. 1976. *Community Activeness and Community Structure*. Ph.D. dissertation in rural sociology. University Park: Penn State University.

Hauser, Philip M. 1965. "Urbanization: An overview." Pp. 1–47 in Philip M. Hauser and Leo F. Schnore (eds.), *The Study of Urbanization*. New York: John Wiley & Sons.

Hawley, Amos. 1944. "Ecology and human ecology." *Social Forces* 22(4):398–405.

Hawley, Amos. 1948. "Discussion." *American Sociological Review* 13(2):153–56.

Hawley, Amos. 1950. *Human Ecology: A Theory of Community Structure*. New York: The Ronald Press Company.

Hawley, Amos. 1971. *Urban Society: An Ecological Approach*. New York: John Wiley & Sons.

Hawley, Amos. 1978. "Urbanization as a process." Pp. 3–26 in David Street and associates (eds.), *Handbook of Contemporary Urban Life*. San Francisco: Jossey-Bass.

Heady, Earl O. 1972. "Elements in making rural development go." Pp. 45–55 in *Increasing Understanding of Public Problems and Policies—1972*. Chicago: The Farm Foundation.

Hennigh, Lawrence. 1978. "The good life and the taxpayers' revolt." *Rural Sociology 43*(2):178–90.

Hiller, E. T. 1941. "The community as a social group." *American Sociological Review 6*(2):189–202.

Hillery, George A., Jr. 1955. "Definitions of community: Areas of agreement." *Rural Sociology 20*(2):111–23.

Hillery, George A. J. 1968. *Communal Organizations: A Study of Local Societies*. Chicago: University of Chicago Press.

Hirschl, Thomas A., and Gene F. Summers. 1982. "Cash transfers and the export base of small communities." *Rural Sociology 47*(2):295–316.

Hock, Irving. 1976. "City size effects trends, and policies." *Science 193*(September):856–63.

Hoiberg, Otto G. 1955. *Exploring the Small Community*. Lincoln: University of Nebraska Press.

Hollingshead, August B. 1948. "Community research: Development and present condition." *American Sociological Review 13*(2):136–48.

Holzner, Burkart. 1967. "The concept 'integration' in sociology." *Sociological Quarterly 8*(1):51–62.

Houghland, James G., Jr., and Willis A. Sutton. 1978. "Factors influencing degree of involvement in interorganizational relationships in a rural county." *Rural Sociology 43*(4):649–70.

Houghland, James G., Jr., Kyong-dong Kim, and James A. Christenson. 1979. "The effects of ecological and socioeconomic status variables on membership and participation in voluntary organizations." *Rural Sociology 44*(3):602–11.

Howes, Candace, and Ann R. Markusen. 1981. "Poverty: A regional political economy perspective." Pp. 437–63 in Amos H. Hawley and Sara Mills Mazie (eds.), *Nonmetropolitan America in Transition*. Chapel Hill: University of North Carolina Press.

Humphrey, Craig R., and Richard S. Krannich. 1980. "The promotion of growth in small urban places and its impact on population change, 1975–78." *Social Science Quarterly 61*(3/4):581–94.

Hunter, Floyd. 1953. *Community Power Structure*. Chapel Hill: University of North Carolina Press.

Israel, Glenn Douglas. 1985. *Community Activeness in New Hampshire Towns*. Ph.D. dissertation in rural sociology. University Park: Pennsylvania State University.

James, William. 1910. *Psychology: The Briefer Course*. New York: Henry Holt & Company.

Johansen, Harley E., and Glenn V. Fuguitt. 1984. *The Changing Rural Village in America: Demographic and Economic Trends Since 1950*. Cambridge, Mass.: Ballinger Publishing Company.

Joint Economic Committee (eds.). 1986. *New Dimensions in Rural Policy: Building Upon Our Heritage*. Washington, D.C.: Congress of the United States (June 5).

Kasarda, John D., and Morris Janowitz. 1974. "Community attachment in mass society." *American Sociological Review* 39(3):328–39.

Katz, Daniel, and Robert L. Kahn. 1966. *The Social Psychology of Organizations*. New York: John Wiley & Sons.

Kaufman, Harold F. 1944. *Prestige Classes in a New York Rural Community*. Ithaca: Cornell University Agricultural Experiment Station Memoir 260.

Kaufman, Harold F. 1959. "Toward an interactional conception of community." *Social Forces* 38(1):8–17.

Kaufman, Harold F. 1985. "An action approach to community development." Pp. 53–65 in Frank A. Fear and Harry K. Schwarzweller (eds.), *Focus on Community*. Volume 2 of Research in Rural Sociology and Development. Greenwich, Conn.: JAI Press.

Kaufman, Harold F., and Kenneth P. Wilkinson. 1967. *Community Structure and Leadership: An Interactional Perspective in the Study of Community*. State College: Mississippi State University Social Science Research Center Bulletin 13.

Keller, Peter A., and J. Dennis Murray (eds.). 1982. *Handbook of Rural Community Mental Health*. New York: Human Sciences Press.

Kolb, J. H. 1923. *Service Relations of Town and Country*. Madison: University of Wisconsin Agricultural Experiment Station Bulletin 58.

Kolb, J. H. 1925. *Service Institutions for Town and Country*. Madison: University of Wisconsin Agricultural Experiment Station Bulletin 66.

Kolb, John H., and Edmund deS. Brunner. 1952. *A Study of Rural Society*. Boston: Houghton Mifflin Company.

Konig, Rene. 1968. *The Community*. Translated by Edward Fitzgerald. New York: Schocken Books.

Kraenzel, Carl F. 1955. *The Great Plains in Transition*. Norman: University of Oklahoma Press.

Kraenzel, Carl F. 1980. *The Social Cost of Space in the Yonland*. Boseman, Mont.: Big Sky Books.

Krannich, Richard S., and Craig R. Humphrey. 1983. "Local mobilization and community growth: Toward an assessment of the 'growth machine' hypothesis." *Rural Sociology* 48(1):60–81.

Krannich, Richard S., Thomas Greider, and Ronald L. Little. 1985. "Rapid growth and fear of crime: A four-community comparison." *Rural Sociology* 50(2):191–207.

Lewis, Oscar. 1948. *On the Edge of the Black Waxy: A Cultural Survey of Bell County, Texas.* St. Louis, Mo.: Washington University Studies New Series, Social and Philosophical Sciences No. 7.

Lloyd, Robert C., and Kenneth P. Wilkinson. 1985. "Community factors in rural manufacturing development." *Rural Sociology* 50(1):27–37.

Loomis, Charles P., and J. Allan Beegle. 1957. "Locality systems." Pp. 22–58 in Charles P. Loomis and J. Allan Beegle, *Rural Sociology: The Strategy of Change.* Englewood Cliffs, N.J.: Prentice-Hall.

Lovejoy, Stephen B., and Richard S. Krannich. 1982. "Rural industrial development and domestic dependency relations: Toward an integrated perspective." *Rural Sociology* 47(3):475–95.

Lukes, Stephen. 1974. *Power: A Radical View.* London: Macmillan.

Luloff, A. E., and Wendy Chittenden. 1984. "Rural industrialization: A logit analysis." *Rural Sociology* 49(1):67–88.

Luloff, A. E., and L. E. Swanson (eds.). 1990. *American Rural Communities.* Boulder, Colo.: Westview Press.

Luloff, A. E., and Kenneth P. Wilkinson. 1979. "Participation in the national flood insurance program: A study of community activeness." *Rural Sociology* 44(1):137–52.

Luloff, A. E., and Kenneth P. Wilkinson. 1990. "Community action and the national rural development agenda." *Sociological Practice* 8:48–57.

Lynd, Robert S., and Helen M. Lynd. 1929. *Middletown: A Study in Contemporary American Culture.* New York: Harcourt, Brace.

Lynd, Robert S., and Helen M. Lynd. 1937. *Middletown in Transition: A Study in Cultural Conflicts.* New York: Harcourt, Brace.

Lyon, Larry, and Charles M. Bonjean. 1981. "Community power and policy outputs: The routines of local politics." *Urban Affairs Quarterly* 17(1):3–21.

McGranahan, David A. 1984. "Local growth and the outside contacts of influentials: An alternative test of the 'growth machine' hypothesis." *Rural Sociology* 49(4):530–40.

MacIver, R. M. 1931. *Community: A Sociological Study, Being an Attempt to Set Out the Nature and Fundamental Laws of Social Life.* New York: Macmillan.

MacIver, R. M., and Charles H. Page. 1949. *Society: An Introductory Analysis.* New York: Rinehart.

Mann, Peter H. 1965. *An Approach to Urban Sociology.* London: Routledge & K. Paul.

Martin, Kenneth E., and Kenneth P. Wilkinson. 1984. "Local participation in the federal grant system: Effects of community action." *Rural Sociology* 49(3):374-88.

Martin, Walter T. 1968. "Theories of variation in the suicide rate." Pp.74-96 in Jack R. Gibbs (ed.), *Suicide*. New York: Harper & Row.

Martindale, Don. 1963. *Community, Character and Civilization*. New York: The Free Press of Glencoe.

Maslow, Abraham H. 1954. *Motivation and Personality*. New York: Harper and Brothers.

Massey, Garth. 1980. "Critical dimensions in urban life: Energy extraction and community collapse in Wyoming." *Urban Life* 9(July):187-99.

Maurer, Richard C., and Ted L. Napier. 1981. "Rural residents' perspectives of industrial development." *Rural Sociology* 46(1):100-11.

Mayhew, Bruce H., and Roger L. Levinger. 1976. "Size and the density of interaction in human aggregates." *American Journal of Sociology* 82(1)86-110.

Mead, George H. 1934. *Mind, Self, and Society: From the Standpoint of a Social Behaviorist*. Edited by Charles W. Morris. Chicago: University of Chicago Press.

Mey, Harold. 1972. *Field-theory: A Study of Its Application in the Social Sciences*. Translated by Douglas Scott. New York: St. Martin's Press.

Micklin, Michael. 1984. "The ecological perspective in the social sciences: A comparative overview." Pp. 51-90 in Michael Micklin and Harvey M. Choldin (eds.), *Sociological Human Ecology: Contemporary Issues and Applications*. Boulder, Colo.: Westview Press.

Miller, Michael K., Donald E. Voth, and Diana Danforth Chapman. 1984. "Estimating the effects of community resource development efforts on county quality of life." *Rural Sociology* 49(1):37-66.

Miller, Paul A. 1953. *Community Health Action*. East Lansing: Michigan State College Press.

Molotch, Harvey. 1976. "The city as a growth machine: Toward a political economy of place." *American Journal of Sociology* 82(2):309-32.

Morgan, Arthur E. 1957. *The Community of the Future: And the Future of Community*. Yellow Springs, Ohio: Community Service.

Morrison, Denton E. 1983. "Soft tech/hard tech, hi tech/lo tech: A social movement analysis of appropriate technology." Pp. 197-216 in Gene F. Summers (ed.), *Technology and Social Change in Rural Areas*. Boulder, Colo.: Westview Press.

Moxley, Robert. 1985. "Vertical assistance, population size, and growth in the context and results of community civic action." *Journal of the Community Development Society* 16(1):57-74.

Mulford, Charles L., and Mary A. Mulford. 1977. "Community and inter-organizational perspectives on cooperation and conflict." *Rural Sociology* 42(4):569–90.

Murdock, Steve, and Willis A. Sutton, Jr. 1974. "The new ecology and community theory: similarities, differences, and convergencies." *Rural Sociology* 39(3):319–33.

Nelson, Joel I., and Robert Grams. 1978. "Worker interaction in occupational communities." *Rural Sociology* 43(2):265–79.

Nelson, Lowry. 1930. "The Mormon village: A study in social origins." *Utah Academy of Sciences* 8:11–37.

Nelson, Lowry. 1952. *The Mormon Village: A Pattern and Technique of Land Settlement.* Salt Lake City: University of Utah Press.

Nelson, Lowry, Charles E. Ramsey, and Coolie Verner. 1960. *Community Structure and Change.* New York: Macmillan.

Newby, Howard. 1980. "Trend report: Rural sociology." *Current Sociology* 28(1):1–141.

Nisbet, Robert A. 1953. *The Quest for Community: A Study in the Ethics of Order and Freedom.* New York: Oxford University Press.

Nix, Harold L., Paula L. Dressel, and Frederick L. Bates. 1977. "Changing leaders and leadership structure: A longitudinal study." *Rural Sociology* 42(1):22–41.

Nowak, Peter J., Roy E. Rickson, Charles E. Ramsey, and Willis J. Goudy. 1982. "Community conflict and models of political participation." *Rural Sociology* 47(2):333–48.

Odum, Howard T. 1970. *Power, Environment and Society.* New York: Wiley-Interscience.

Ogden, Jean, and Jess Ogden. 1946. *Small Communities in Action: Stories of Citizen Programs at Work.* New York: Harper and Brothers.

Olson, Phillip. 1964. "Rural American community studies: The survival of public ideology." *Human Organization* 23(4):342–50.

Olsson, Gunnar. 1965. *Distance and Human Interaction: A Review and Bibliography.* Philadelphia: Regional Science Research Institute Biography Series Number Two.

Osborne, J. Grayson, William Boyle, and Walter R. Borg. 1984. "Rapid community growth and the problems of elementary and secondary students." *Rural Sociology* 49(4):553–567.

Pahl, R. E. 1966. "The rural–urban continuum." *Sociologia Ruralis* 6(3/4):299–326.

Park, Robert E., Ernest W. Burgess, and Roderick D. McKenzie. 1925. *The City.* Chicago: University of Chicago Press.

Parsons, Talcott. 1951. *The Social System.* Glencoe, Ill.: The Free Press.

Parsons, Talcott. 1960. *Structure and Process in Modern Societies.* Glencoe, Ill.: The Free Press.

Parsons, Talcott. 1966. *Societies: Evolutionary and Comparative Perspectives.* Englewood Cliffs, N.J.: Prentice-Hall.

Plant, Raymond. 1974. *Community and Ideology: An Essay in Applied Social Philosophy.* London: Routledge and Kegan Paul.

Ploch, Louis A. 1976. "Community development in action: A case study." *Journal of the Community Development Society* 7(1):5–16.

Ploch, Louis A. 1989. *Landaff—Then and Now.* Orono: University of Maine Agricultural Experiment Station Bulletin 828.

Poole, Dennis. 1981. "Farm scale, family life, and community participation." *Rural Sociology* 46(1):112–27.

Poplin, Dennis E. 1979. *Communities: A Survey of Theories and Methods of Research.* Second edition. New York: Macmillan.

Preston, James C. 1983. "Patterns in nongovernmental community action in small communities." *Journal of the Community Development Society* 14(2):83–94.

Preston, James D., and Patricia B. Guseman. 1979. "A comparison of the findings of different methods for identifying community leaders." *Journal of the Community Development Society* 10(2):51–62.

Price, Michael L., and Daniel C. Clay. 1980. "Structural disturbances in rural communities: Some repercussions of the migration turnaround in Michigan." *Rural Sociology* 45(4):591–607.

Rank, Mark R., and Paul R. Voss. 1982. "Patterns of rural community involvement: A comparison of residents and recent immigrants." *Rural Sociology* 47(2):197–219.

Redfield, Robert. 1955. *The Little Community. Viewpoints for the Study of a Human Whole.* Chicago: University of Chicago Press.

Reiss, Albert J., Jr. 1959. "The sociological study of communities." *Rural Sociology* 24(2):118–130.

Richards, Robert O. 1978. "Urbanization of rural areas." Pp. 551–91 in David Street and associates (eds.), *Handbook of Contemporary Urban Life.* San Francisco: Jossey-Bass.

Robinson, Jerry W., Jr. 1989. "The conflict approach." Pp. 80–116 in James A. Christenson and Jerry W. Robinson, Jr. (eds.), *Community Development in Perspective.* Ames: Iowa State University Press.

Rogers, David L., Brian F. Pendleton, Willis J. Goudy, and Robert O. Richards. 1978. "Industrialization, income benefits, and the rural community." *Rural Sociology* 43(2):250–64.

Ryan, William. 1971. *Blaming the Victim.* New York: Vintage Books.

Sanders, Irwin T. 1950. *Making Good Communities Better: A Handbook for Civic-Minded Men and Women.* Lexington: University of Kentucky Press.

Sanders, Irwin T. 1958. "Theories of community development." *Rural Sociology* 23(1):1–12.

Sanders, Irwin T. 1966. *The Community: An Introduction to a Social System*. New York: The Ronald Press Company.

Sanders, Irwin T., and Gordon F. Lewis. 1976. "Rural community studies in the United States: A decade in review." *Annual Review of Sociology* 2:35–53.

Sanderson, Dwight, and Robert Polson. 1939. *Rural Community Organization*. New York: John Wiley & Sons.

Saunders, Peter, Howard Newby, Colin Bell, and David Rose. 1978. "Rural community and rural community power." Pp. 55–85 in Howard Newby (ed.), *International Perspectives in Rural Sociology*. Chichester, England: John Wiley & Sons.

Scherer, Jacqueline. 1972. *Contemporary Community: Sociological Illusion or Reality?* London: Tavistock.

Schmalenbach, Herman. 1961. "The sociological category of communion." Pp. 331–47 in Vol. 1 of Talcott Parsons, Edward Shils, Kaspar D. Naegele, and Jesse R. Pitts (eds.), *Theories of Society: Foundations of Modern Sociological Theory*. New York: The Free Press of Glencoe.

Schroeder, W. Widick, and J. Allan Beegle. 1953. "Suicide: An instance of high rural rates." *Rural Sociology* 18(March):45–52.

Schumacher, E. F. 1973. *Small is Beautiful: Economics as if People Mattered*. New York: Harper & Row.

Shils, Edward. 1972. *The Intellectuals and the Powers, and Other Essays*. Chicago: University of Chicago Press.

Simmel, Georg. 1950. "The metropolis and mental life." Pp. 409–24 in Kurt H. Wolff, *The Sociology of Georg Simmel*. Translated by H.H. Gerth and C. Wright Mills. New York: The Free Press of Glencoe.

Sims, Newell L. 1912. *A Hoosier Village: A Sociological Study with Special Reference to Social Causation*. New York: Longmans, Green.

Smith, Suzanne M. 1970. *An Annotated Bibliography of Small Town Research*. Madison: University of Wisconsin Department of Rural Sociology.

Snipp, C. Matthew, and Gene F. Summers. 1981. "The welfare state in the community: A general model and empirical assessment." *Rural Sociology* 46(4):582–607.

Sofranko, Andrew J., and Frederick C. Fliegel. 1984. "Dissatisfaction with satisfaction." *Rural Sociology* 49(3):353–73.

Sorokin, Pitirim A. 1929. "Rural–urban suicides." Pp. 171–80 in Pitirim A. Sorokin and Carle C. Zimmerman, *Principles of Rural–Urban Sociology*. New York: Henry Holt.

Sorokin, Pitirim A., and Carle C. Zimmerman. 1929. *Principles of Rural-Urban Sociology*. New York: Henry Holt.

Sorokin, Pitirim A., Carle C. Zimmerman, and Charles J. Galpin. 1930. *A Systematic Source Book in Rural Sociology*. Minneapolis: University of Minnesota Press.

Stack, Steven. 1982. "Suicide: A decade review of the sociological literature." *Deviant Behavior* 4(October-November):41-66.

Stein, Maurice. 1960. *The Eclipse of Community: An Interpretation of American Studies*. Princeton, N.J.: Princeton University Press.

Summers, Gene F. 1986. "Rural community development." *Annual Review of Sociology* 12:341-71.

Sutton, Willis A., Jr., and Jiri Kolaja. 1960a. "Elements of community action." *Social Forces* 38(4):325-31.

Sutton, Willis A,. Jr., and Jiri Kolaja. 1960b. "The concept of community." *Rural Sociology* 25(2):197-203.

Till, Thomas E. 1981. "Manufacturing industry: Trends and impacts." Pp. 194-230 in Amos H. Hawley and Sara Mills Mazie (eds.), *Nonmetropolitan America in Transition*. Chapel Hill: University of North Carolina Press.

Tilly, Charles. 1973. "Do communities act?" *Sociological Inquiry* 43(3/4):209-40.

Toennies, Ferdinand. 1957. *Community and Society*. Translated and edited by Charles P. Loomis. East Lansing: Michigan State University Press.

Trout, Deborah L. 1980. "The role of social isolation in suicide." *Suicide and Life-threatening Behavior* 10(Spring):10-23.

Turney-High, Harry Holbert. 1968. *Man and System: Foundations for the Study of Human Relations*. New York: Appleton-Century-Crofts.

Vidich, Arthur J., and Joseph Bensman. 1958. *Small Town in Mass Society: Class, Power and Religion in a Rural Community*. Princeton, N.J.: Princeton University Press.

Vogt, Evon Z., and Thomas F. O'Dea. 1953. "A comparative study of the role of values in social action in two southwestern communities." *American Sociological Review* 18(6):645-54.

Voth, Donald E., Michael K. Miller, and James Flaherty. 1982. "The impact of differential communications structures on rural community development efforts." *Journal of the Community Development Society* 13(1):43-57.

Wagenfeld, Morton O. 1982. "Psychopathology in rural areas: Issues and evidence." Pp. 30-44 in P.A. Keller and J.D. Murray (eds.), *Handbook of Rural Community Mental Health*. New York: Human Sciences Press.

132

References

Walker, Richard A. 1978. "Two sources of uneven development under advanced capitalism: Spatial differentiation and capital mobility." *Review of Radical Political Economics* 10(3):28–37.

Walton, John. 1976. "Community power and the retreat from politics: Full circle after twenty years?" *Social Problems* 23(3):292–303.

Warner, Paul D., and Rabel J. Burdge. 1979. "Perceived adequacy of community services." *Rural Sociology* 44(2):392–400.

Warner, W. Keith. 1974. "Rural society in a post-industrial age." *Rural Sociology* 39(3):306–18.

Warner, W. Lloyd, and Paul S. Lunt. 1941. *The Social Life of a Modern Community*. New Haven: Yale University Press.

Warren, Roland L. 1978. *The Community in America*. Third edition. Chicago: Rand McNally.

Webber, Melvin. 1964. "Order in diversity: Community without propinquity." Pp. 23–54 in Lowdon Wingo (ed.), *Cities and Space: The Future of Urban Land*. Baltimore: Johns Hopkins University Press.

Wellman, Barry. 1979. "The community question: The intimate networks of East Yorkers." *American Journal of Sociology* 84(5):1201–31.

Wellman, Barry, and Barry Leighton. 1979. "Networks, neighborhoods, and communities: Approaches to the study of the community question." *Urban Affairs Quarterly* 14(3):363–90.

West, James. 1945. *Plainville, U.S.A.* New York: Columbia University Press.

Whiting, Larry R. (ed.). 1974. *Communities Left Behind: Alternatives for Development*. Ames: Iowa State University Press.

Wilkinson, Kenneth P. 1969. "Special agency program accomplishment and community action styles: The case of watershed development." *Rural Sociology* 34(1):29–42.

Wilkinson, Kenneth P. 1970a. "Phases and roles in community action." *Rural Sociology* 35(1):54–68.

Wilkinson, Kenneth P. 1970b. "The community as a social field." *Social Forces* 48(3):311–22.

Wilkinson, Kenneth P. 1972. "A field-theory perspective for community development research." *Rural Sociology* 37(1):43–52.

Wilkinson, Kenneth P. 1973. "Sociological concepts of social well-being: Frameworks for evaluation of water resources projects." Pp. 160–70 in Wade H. Andrews, Rabel J. Burdge, Harold R. Capener, W. Keith Warner and Kenneth P. Wilkinson (eds.), *The Social Well-Being and Quality of Life Dimension in Water Resources Planning and Development*. Logan, Utah: University Council on Water Resources.

Wilkinson, Kenneth P. 1974. "A behavioral approach to measurement and analysis of community field structure." *Rural Sociology* 39(2):247-56.

Wilkinson, Kenneth P. 1979. "Social well-being and community." *Journal of the Community Development Society* 10(1):5-16.

Wilkinson, Kenneth P. 1984a. "Implementing a national strategy of rural development." *The Rural Sociologist* 4(5):348-53.

Wilkinson, Kenneth P. 1984b. "Rurality and patterns of social disruption." *Rural Sociology* 49(1):23-36.

Wilkinson, Kenneth P. 1986a. "Communities left behind—again." Pp. 341-46 in Joint Economic Committee (ed.), *New Dimensions in Rural Policy: Building Upon Our Heritage*. Washington, D.C.: Congress of the United States (June 5).

Wilkinson, Kenneth P. 1986b. "In search of the community in the changing countryside." *Rural Sociology* 51(1):1-17.

Wilkinson, Kenneth P. 1988. "The community crisis in the rural South." Pp. 72-86 in Lionel J. Beaulieu (ed.), *The Rural South in Crisis: Challenges for the Future*. Boulder, Colo.: Westview Press.

Wilkinson, Kenneth P. 1989. "Community development and industrial policy." Pp. 241-54 in William W. Falk and Thomas A. Lyson (eds.), *A Focus on Rural Labor Markets*. Vol. 3 of Research in Rural Sociology and Rural Development. Greenwich, Conn.: JAI Press.

Wilkinson, Kenneth P., and Glenn D. Israel. 1984. "Suicide and rurality in urban society." *Suicide and Life-threatening Behavior* 14(3):187-200.

Wilkinson, Kenneth P., Michael J. Camasso, and A. E. Luloff. 1984. "Nonmetropolitan participation in programs of the Great Society." *Social Science Quarterly* 65(4):1092-1103.

Wilkinson, Kenneth P., James G. Thompson, Robert R. Reynolds, Jr., and Lawrence M. Ostresh. 1982. "Local social disruption and western energy development." *Pacific Sociological Review* 25(3):275-95.

Williams, Anne S. 1980. "Relationships between the structure of local influence and policy outcomes." *Rural Sociology* 45(4):621-43.

Williams, James M. 1906. *An American Town: A Sociological Study*. New York: James Kempster.

Willits, Fern K., and Robert C. Bealer. 1967. "An evaluation of a composite definition of 'rurality.' " *Rural Sociology* 32(2):165-77.

Willits, Fern K., Robert C. Bealer, and Donald M. Crider. 1982. "Persistence of rural/urban differences." Pp. 69-76 in Don A. Dillman and Daryl J. Hobbs (eds.), *Rural Society in the U.S.: Issues for the 1980s*. Boulder, Colo.: Westview Press.

Wilson, Warren H. 1907. *Quaker Hill: A Sociological Study*. New York: Columbia University.

Wirth, Louis. 1938. "Urbanism as a way of life." *American Journal of Sociology* 44(1):1–24.

Yinger, J. Milton. 1965. *Toward a Field Theory of Behavior: Personality and Social Structure.* New York: McGraw-Hill.

Zimmerman, Carle C. 1938. *The Changing Community.* New York: Harper & Brothers.

Zuiches, James J. 1981. "Residential preferences in the United States." Pp. 72–115 in Amos H. Hawley and Sara Mills Mazie (eds.), *Nonmetropolitan America in Transition.* Chapel Hill: University of North Carolina Press.

Index

ABOUT THE AUTHOR

KENNETH P. WILKINSON is Professor of Rural Sociology at Pennsylvania State University. He has written extensively on rural and community development, policy issues, social dysfunction in rural areas, and related topics.

**Recent Titles in
Contributions in Sociology**

Population and Community in Rural America
Lorraine Garkovich

Divided We Stand: Class Structure in Israel from 1948 to the 1980s
Amir Ben-Porat

A Fragile Movement: The Struggle for Neighborhood Stabilization
Juliet Saltman

The Sociology of Agriculture
Frederick H. Buttel, Olaf F. Larson, and Gilbert W. Gillespie, Jr.

The Urban Housing Crisis: Economic, Social, and Legal Issues and
Proposals
Arlene Zarembka

Time, Memory, and Society
Franco Ferrarotti

Homelessness in the United States. Volume II: Data and Issues
Jamshid A. Momeni, editor

Promises in the Promised Land: Mobility and Inequality in Israel
Vered Kraus and Robert W. Hodge

Switzerland in Perspective
Janet Eve Hilowitz, editor

Rethinking Today's Minorities
Vincent N. Parrillo, editor

Beyond Ethnocentrism: A Reconstruction of Marx's Concept of Science
Charles McKelvey